The
BREATH
of
GOD

From Our Emptiness to His Fullness...

The BREATH *of* GOD

From Our Emptiness to His Fullness…

IRMA ELIZABETH DIAZ

Treasure House

An Imprint of
Destiny Image® Publishers, Inc.
P.O. Box 310
Shippensburg, PA 17257-0310

"For where your treasure is, there will your heart be also."
Matthew 6:21

ISBN 0-7684-3025-9

For Worldwide Distribution
Printed in the U.S.A.

This book and all other Destiny Image, Revival Press, MercyPlace, Fresh Bread, and Treasure House books are available at Christian bookstores and distributors worldwide.

For a U.S. bookstore nearest you, call **1-800-722-6774**.
For more information on foreign distributors, call **717-532-3040**.
Or reach us on the Internet: **http://www.reapernet.com**

DEDICATION

I dedicate this book first to my beloved YHWH, "I AM THAT I AM" (Ex. 3:14), who gives the burning bush experience.

> *"You have captured my soul with Your fullness."*

To my parents, Daniel and Velia Diaz.

> *"Because of your unselfish love and support,*
> *many will be revolutionized through all your seed."*

To my children, Albert, Christina, and Jeannette.

To my grandchildren, Julian, Simon, Juliette, and those unborn generations yet to come.

> *"You are a gift from God sheltered in His shadow;*
> *the fruit of my labor shall be upon you."*

ACKNOWLEDGMENTS

To all those whom God has used to birth *The Breath of God*, and to all my ministry partners for their commitment to establish that which God has set in motion through Upon This Rock Ministries—with all my heart I express my appreciation.

MY MINISTRY TEAM

To my precious armorbearer and friend Wanda Calime, who continually upholds me with her heart in prayers and service to the Lord. Thank you for standing with me. May your dreams be fulfilled.

To Renee Kwiecinski for her commitment to excellence and many hours of administrative work, and to Irene and Albert Ortiz for their diligence in event planning and development. To Carolyn Arevalos, Anthony Calime, Vedie and Felix Daclan, Rich Kwiecinski, Sylvia Leierer, Maria and Carlos Longoria, Rebecca Longoria, Jann Mathies, Judy and Alan Sproull, Cynthia Vega, Cheri Walter, Gail Young and Brandon Young. Thank you for your love, your prayers, and your willingness to hold up my arms. You caught the vision with me and it was written, that all who read it may run with it.

To Pastor Danny Diaz (my precious brother), Senior Pastor of Victorious Living Christian Center in Pomona, California. Thank you for your many prayers for me. They avail much.

To Pastor Ken Clowdus, Senior Pastor of Community Christian Center in Covina, California, for your sound counsel and prayers. To your 5 a.m. prayer group who pray for me daily—thank you.

To Joseph Baruch Shulam, Director of Netiviyah Bible Instruction Ministry in Jerusalem, Israel. Your friendship is invaluable to me.

LAUNCHING THE PROJECT

To Lonnie Beck, Darlene Delange, Donna Ferguson, Betty Hawkins and Jo Kadlecek for helping me launch this eternal work. Thank you for your obedience and faithfulness. To all the staff at Destiny Image for seeing with the eye of the Spirit. You knew me before you met me. May the Lord cause the seed you sowed to flourish beyond your expectation.

To Sandi Swanson and the Eleventh Hour Television Ministry for always sharing your platform with me. Blessings be upon you!

To Dan Joseph of Victorious Productions and Kim Murray of Vision Media, thank you for standing with me.

A SPECIAL EXPRESSION OF APPRECIATION

To Pastors John and Rita Calderon, Senior Pastors of New Home Foursquare Church in Los Banos, California, where *The Breath of God* was birthed on a Sunday morning in the fall of 1998.

THANK YOU ALL

May the Lord breathe His fullness upon all of you and may you be endowed with enabling grace and fire to step out on the edge for my Beloved. I love you and appreciate you. You are all gifts from God for me.

ENDORSEMENTS

"Irma has a unique balance of ministry. She is anointed of God in delivery and is studied in her presentation of the Word. She submits to the leadership she is serving. I appreciate her ministry and treasure our friendship. *The Breath of God* is required reading."

Cliff Traub, Executive Presbyter
Northern California/Nevada Assemblies of God, and
Senior Pastor, Bethel Church
Modesto, California

"Reverend Irma has a powerful anointing on her life and ministry. She is an individual of integrity, humility, and strength. She speaks with great authority that can only result from long hours in the presence of Jehovah! She shared her recent findings on Ruach Ha Kodesh with my congregation. What an incredible revelation of the Spirit of God and how He wants to breathe on His Church today! It was a fresh and much needed word from the throne of God and has revolutionized our thoughts on the Holy Spirit of God! This discovery is such a powerful and mighty word that will greatly benefit the Body of Christ."

Todd Smith, Senior Pastor
The Rock Christian Fellowship
Gainesville, Georgia

"The Bible is filled with revelation and Irma Diaz is filled with the Bible. The insight delivered on a Sunday morning at our church was timely, revelatory and directional. God is searching for congregations in two areas, response and behavior. The fullness of God (Ruach Ha Kodesh) is the cry of every ministry desirous of an uncontaminated move of God. Irma Diaz's ministry of passion/compassion is rooted in the building, loving, and prophetic unveiling that God's people can possess! She is a friend of a pastor."

Glen Berteau, Senior Pastor
Calvary Temple Worship Center
Modesto, California

"In every generation God raises up individuals to be His voice, and to speak His *rhema* word for that hour. I sincerely believe Irma Diaz to be one of those individuals whom God has raised up to speak into this generation the rhema word of God! Irma's revelation and insight into Ruach Ha Kodesh (the Breath of God) is crisp, fresh, and relevant to the times in which we live. I think every believer needs to be exposed to this sound revelation/truth as I believe it to be pertinent to what God is doing in this present hour! It has been my privilege to host the Reverend Irma Diaz on several occasions at Christian Life Center in Merced, California. I have become well acquainted with her as an individual and a minister of the Gospel. I have always found her to be sound and well studied. God has placed a special cutting-edge anointing upon her that causes her message to come forth in a freshness that penetrates deeply into the hearts of the hearers."

Randy Bissell, Senior Pastor
Christian Life Center
Merced, California

"To every woman of God, Irma Diaz stands out powerfully as a mighty example who is not afraid to unleash all the power and promises of the living Lord in her life and the lives of those she touches through her ministry."

Major Nancy Banfield
Salvation Army
Women's Ministries Secretary, Eastern Territorial Headquarters
Nyack, New York

CONTENTS

INTRODUCTION

"CATCHING" HOLD OF GOD

Perhaps because of my parents' sincere devotion to their Catholic faith and the way they lived it out in our large, close-knit Hispanic family, my young spirit was especially alive and responsive. At five years old, I'd climb the grassy hill up the street from my house in Los Angeles, where I was born and raised, and sit on the abandoned railroad tracks. There, staring at the beauty around me, I sat and talked with God. Sometimes I'd roll around in the grass and tell God how much I loved Him, how beautiful I thought He was, and how much I wanted to see Him. At other times I'd jump up in the air and try to "catch" Him, like a child tries to touch her tall father. When I couldn't go up to the hill to talk to God, I sat in the pews at church and pretended I was jumping up to catch Him. I might have been only five years old, but I knew without a doubt that I loved God.

I remember one day in particular when, as I was up on the hill playing and trying to "catch" God, I suddenly began to cry. Soon I was weeping, my little shoulders shaking, as I sobbed for what seemed a very long time. It wasn't a cry of sadness or of burdens, but a good cry, the kind that "filled me up" rather than emptying me out. I wasn't afraid; I knew God was there, settling upon me like a big hug. I felt so happy and loved, but I wasn't sure what to do with that wonderful

Presence, so I just sat and cried. Then, all of a sudden, I jumped up, running and laughing, unable to contain the joy that overflowed me. Although I was too young to understand it then, I know now that what I experienced that day was my first glorious, personal encounter with the Breath of God. But one thing I did know, even at that tender age: God loved me, and He would never, ever leave me—a truth I never forgot, regardless of my age or the circumstances of my life.

Since then, as an adult, I've had the privilege of working in the political arena for several years, where I learned some valuable truths and insights and met many interesting and influential people. But it was God's Spirit, whispering to mine, that brought about the transition in my life from politics to full-time ministry. His words to me were, "You can change legislation, elect the righteous to government, and incarcerate the perpetrators, but if you do not bring them Jesus, you have labored in vain. I have called you to bring My Son. I have called you to work for Me. Behold, I do a new thing."

The message was so clear that I soon had a peace about the many adjustments I would have to make in my life in order to answer this call of God. The obstacles and frustrations involved in such a major change of direction were numerous, but the peace remained, and soon I was ministering in a way I would never have dreamed possible apart from God's personal word of calling and anointing upon my life. And so began Upon This Rock Ministries, a three-pronged ministry that is:

- *Prophetic:* Being used of God to set in motion His message of the hour;

- *Apostolic:* Establishing that which has been set in motion by God and building the local church;

- *Evangelistic:* Building a solid outreach to souls from all walks of life.

As I continually studied these three aspects of ministry, I became more and more intrigued with the concept of the Breath of God and the fullness of the Godhead. Those studies, along with my ever-growing times of "catching" God in communion and prayer, led to a greater understanding of the *Ruach Ha Kodesh* (Roo'-akh ha Ko'-desh: Hebrew for the Holy Spirit, literally, "Holy or Sacred Breath or Blast") and, eventually, to the birthing of this book.

CATCHING THE SPIRIT

I have always been intrigued by the Holy Spirit because He seemed like the "mother" in the family. We have the Father and Son, and then the Holy Spirit, who often seems to display or represent the maternal qualities in the Godhead. I'd always been drawn to the nurturing and tender love of the Spirit, so seeking or studying Him became an ongoing pursuit. I read every book, studied every passage of Scripture on the Holy Spirit and God's fullness, watched godly men and women operate in the Spirit, and prayed continually for understanding. I was beginning to realize that the Spirit of God encompasses everything that our covenant with God represents.

Soon I began to speak of the Father and Son together in one Spirit as the Breath of God. His Spirit is omnipotent (all powerful) and omnipresent (everywhere); however, there is a difference between the omnipotent, omnipresent, merciful God of the covenant, who gave His only Son to save us and woos us by His Spirit, and the manifested (revealed) Breath of God being sent our way.

Due to the different renderings of Christian and rabbinical theology, those of us in the Church have sometimes found ourselves clouded and, consequently, limited in our understanding of the Spirit of God. Scripture reveals the full attributes of God's Spirit—that is, being endued (covered, saturated, clothed) with power (see Lk. 24:49), the spirit of prophecy (see Rev. 19:10), and the anointing that destroys every yoke of bondage (see Is. 10:27). The Hebrew term for God's Spirit—Ruach Ha Kodesh—encompasses, within its meaning, that same fullness of the attributes of the Spirit of God. Beginning to understand and lay hold of (or "catch") this fullness of God's Spirit revolutionizes our personal walk with God, our ministry, and everything we say, do, or touch.

Discovering these truths about the fullness of God caused me to press in even more to His Holy Spirit for revelation of God's Word. I knew there were human limitations to our capacity to understand God (see Deut. 29:29), but I also realized there was yet so much I longed to learn and, in turn, teach to others. Such desire within me made me listen all the more, as He began to speak to me about the fullness of His Spirit.

Through the years I have asked the question many times as to why certain generations, people, churches, and cities have been graced with revival or social righteousness, while others have not. I also have wondered about some of our great heroes of the faith at the turn of the century. In fact, from biblical days through the nineteenth century, these heroes were selected by God to perform wondrous works. But the more I thought about it, the more I asked, "What did they have that we don't?"

I know I'm not the only one asking those questions. There are pastors sitting in their offices today, wondering why revival has not come to their church or city. They grieve over not seeing people rise up out of wheelchairs or be healed from long-term illnesses, or their congregations not growing in numbers and in spiritual maturity. Finally, I've begun to understand that such questions are birthed out of a lack of understanding of the fullness of God.

GOD'S BREATH

I believe that to have Ruach Ha Kodesh in our lives is to experience all degrees of prophecy, or God's fullness. Ruach Ha Kodesh graces generations, individuals, cities, and local companies of believers. Because Ruach Ha Kodesh is Breath, then it stands to reason that the Breath must be sent by the One breathing. If I blow my breath on you, I deliberately want to send it to you. When I preach, I am deliberately sending my breath your way.

Ruach Ha Kodesh is the fullness of the Godhead, encompassing all the deity of God. Ruach Ha Kodesh is all in all, the great "I AM" (see Ex. 3:14): Father, Son, and Holy Ghost. When I think of my *Abba* (Hebrew term of endearment, meaning "Daddy"), or Father God, I think about the Creator of the universe, a loving God who will not lie to me or let me down, One who is all-encompassing and has a plan and an answer for everything. He is the Creator, the One who creates, from nothing, all things. He is my Father, and He is the All-Powerful One. He is the Covenant Maker. There is nothing that compares with Him.

When I think about Jesus, Emmanuel (God with us), I think about the Lamb of God, slain from the foundation of the earth, the Lion of the Tribe of Judah. He is the victorious Redeemer. He is my

Beloved, and I am His. He is my everything. In Him are all of God's promises fulfilled. In Him is eternal life. In Him is miracle power for signs and wonders. In Him is compassion and love. Everything became available to us through Him who became our Covenant.

The more I discovered of God's Breath and character, the more Scriptures confirmed my findings. In Ephesians 3, the apostle Paul prayed for the Church,

> *That Christ may dwell in your hearts by faith; that ye, being rooted and grounded in love, may be able to comprehend with all saints what is the breadth, and length, and depth, and height; and to know the love of Christ, which passeth knowledge, that ye might be filled with all the fulness of God* (Ephesians 3:17-19).

The meaning of the word *comprehend* in this verse is "surpassing knowledge." This passage speaks of understanding in dimensions: breadth, length, depth, and height. The dimensions used are very similar to the dimensions I would utilize to describe the Breath of God and the glory of God. Those dimensions are without limitations. "For this cause," Paul wrote in verse 14, "I bow my knees [and pray for you, that you would be strong and rooted and grounded in holy, redeeming love]." Why did the apostle pray that way? Because God fell in love with us first. (See 1 John 4:19.) We must endeavor to grasp or "catch" the dimensions of this redeeming love, although we will never fully do so because it exceeds anything we are capable of imagining. God's love runs so much deeper than the depths of hell, for it is a holy love, reaching the Holy of Holies and finding itself higher than the heavens. It is never-ending, from everlasting to everlasting.

Although mentioned first in the dimensions but last here in a place of honor, the breadth of God's love reaches every social and economic status, every university, every motion picture studio, every prison cell, and every obscure corner of the earth. It is unique because it reaches all time, to every age and generation. It cannot be limited and has no parameters. In fact, the clock, the computer, or our human mind cannot begin to compete with the breadth of His love.

The breadth of God, as the Love of God, will find each of us. To understand or apprehend this, Paul prayed that we might not look for the breadth or love of God in the form of knowledge but rather in comprehension. Speaking in spiritual terms, to have knowledge is to grasp with the mind; to comprehend is to grasp with the heart. This is yet another dimension of revelation. To know or "catch" hold of this love of God is to surpass knowledge and be filled with God's fullness. To have the fullness of God is to have been breathed upon by Ruach Ha Kodesh. This Sacred Breath contains the divine fullness of God. It is my conviction that God desires to breathe His fullness upon His Church in this day.

Once we confess with our heart and mouth that Jesus Christ is Lord (see Rom. 10:9-10), we enter His divine covenant of grace. Then, once we truly begin to "walk after His divine Presence," we receive from Ruach Ha Kodesh an enabling grace to go beyond good works, an empowering to pour out grace as He does. It is a "walking after God."

For the past six years I have shared these insights with Christians from all walks of life. Together we have seen that to have the fullness of the Godhead brings an enabling grace to operate as stewards of the mysteries of God (see 1 Cor. 4:1); to see miracles, signs, and wonders; and to acknowledge that, first, there must be grace poured out upon— and by—us. It is the Ruach Ha Kodesh who enables us to do that.

In summary, Ruach Ha Kodesh is the anointing of enabling grace that contains the fullness of the Godhead, which is all the attributes of the Trinity: Father, Son, and Holy Spirit. That fullness, or Breath of God, illuminates, creates, and restores all who come into its path. Is it possible that a human can "catch" that fullness and contain it? With that question in mind, our journey begins....

Chapter 1

CATCHING ON FIRE:
The Breath of God *Illuminating*

Something happened to me in the past few years of my walk with God. Somewhere along the line I "caught on fire." For me to say that might seem odd, as my cup has always run over with passion for God. But it's as if I've had a "conversion within the conversion."

It would be inaccurate to speak of this "conversion within the conversion" as a one-time event. It was more like a series of very identifiable occurrences. During intimate moments in study and on the platform in the middle of ministry to others, I felt a "blaze" coming upon me. It was evident that something was happening, but I didn't quite understand what it was. Comments regarding the apparent change in my life came frequently, primarily from those who came to greet me after I'd ministered somewhere, people who didn't know my everyday walk but who followed the ministry from place to place. It was obvious to them that I had "caught on fire" and was ablaze with the love and presence of God.

INSPIRATION IN THE FIRE OF ILLUMINATION

When I consider the fire of God, I am reminded of the Old Testament altars of sacrifice and how the fire on the altar was to remain burning at all times. (See Leviticus 6:13.) Figuratively and biblically speaking, this fire represents divine inspiration that comes only through God's presence. When divine inspiration is given or imparted, it is like an inhaling or "breathing in" of divine influence. This does not speak of illumination, per se, but rather of a supernatural infusion or influence that enables someone to know truth. God gives this divine inspiration to take us to another level *inside* of us before it is evident *outside*. As God takes us to that new level on the inside, we find ourselves inspired by things we may have known for years, possibly a Scripture that never jumped off the page before but suddenly comes alive. This is God's divine influence penetrating our soul, and it is like fire.

In the past few years, I've experienced this divine inspiration exerted upon all three areas of my soul: my mind, will, and emotions. I've become aroused and excited about the things of God. It's as though I've inhaled the very Breath of God.

Why do some people within the Church experience this divine inspiration of God, while others don't? Why is it, in fact, that so many within the Body of Christ seem to have no fire at all? I know that when I'm divinely inspired I feel as if I can walk through a wall. However, when I'm not, everything looks dreadfully difficult. The things I've learned and heard through the years no longer do anything for me. The pastor is not "cutting it," the worship seems flat, the altar calls uninviting. How does that happen? How do I *allow* this to happen in my life? How does anyone?

Might I suggest that we *all* must get to a place where we are *impelled* with what we have already learned and experienced? We must burn for what we already know, and then more will come.

When I speak of someone who is "divinely inspired," I am not referring to the immature, zealous, off-balance Christian who refuses to be accountable to leadership. That is not the fire of divine inspiration. God is a God of order. (See First Corinthians 14:40.) When I refer to divinely inspired people, I speak of those truly submitted to where God has planted them and who are growing and bearing fruit as they are pruned. There is nothing wrong with seeking more from God, but not at the risk of neglecting "the Rock from which we were hewn"—that which has already become truth. (See Isaiah 51:1.)

To be divinely inspired is to submit to the purging of the Lord. This reminds me of Jeremiah 18, when the Lord told the prophet to go to the potter's house to hear God's voice. Because Jeremiah wanted to hear from God, he immediately obeyed. A prophet must be inspired in order to prophesy, but to be inspired he must first hear from God. We, like Jeremiah, must get to a place where we desire to hear from God and are willing to do whatever He directs in order to receive a word from Him.

When this divine inspiration comes upon us, it is accompanied by a tenacity to improve our spiritual walk. We begin to examine areas in our life we never before thought needed to be examined. When we have been divinely inspired, even when it means facing a spiritual struggle, something inside us refuses to give up. And when we have heard from God, we become candidates for additional degrees of illumination. We find ourselves having "ears to hear" (see Mt. 11:15) as never before. To be divinely inspired is to have been breathed upon by the One who is our God. (See John 20:21-22.) Divine inspiration is contained within the fire of God, and it is attainable to each of us. That divine inspiration is the first degree of the fire of God, and it illuminates everything that touches our lives, whether new revelation or long-known facts. And it is only released by the Breath of the fullness of God, the Ruach Ha Kodesh.

SPIRITUAL POWER IN THE FIRE OF ILLUMINATION

This fire of God also represents spiritual power. This power brings about an ability to produce (the Jews might say "to perform"). It is as though that which is inhaled (Holy Breath) must be exhaled. This would actually cause one to become *as* the Breath of God. Let me explain.

While on a recent trip to the East Coast in the United States, the Lord began to minister to me about being His Breath. In other words, as His stewards of the Word, we become "sent breath." When we are inspired, we have taken in a divine influence that, once responded to, will cause a need within us to convey it to others. As did the prophet Jeremiah, we must now *exhale*.

This inspiration becomes an ability, a strength, an actual force. In other words, this inspiration becomes spiritual power. We suddenly are carriers of something divine. This is where the anointing of God becomes recognizable, even to the heathen. Spiritual power from God, released through our lives, gives us an anointing to step into our call with a surety that turns the hearts of mankind, making an impact on all around us. In fact, there have been times when I've had a message burning inside me with such intensity that I felt as if I would burst if I couldn't release it. I liken that to "holding my breath." To get release, I must exhale!

To bring balance to this picture, I must emphasize that the spirit of the prophet is subject to the prophet. (See First Corinthians 14:32.) In other words, we can and should hold a message from God until the appropriate time. When Jeremiah refused to prophesy, he said it was like fire shut up in his bones. (See Jeremiah 20:9.) He was *compelled* to speak. However, Jeremiah was functioning as a prophet *in the office of a prophet* (see Eph. 4:11), with the authority and anointing to set in motion direction for God's people at that hour. This is different than when we are sitting in the local church, feeling the fire of God stirring within us a message to bring to the assembly. When that happens, we must wait for God to present the proper time for the message to be delivered. "Feeling the fire" does not give us license to usurp authority in a place of worship.

Spiritual power, birthed through divine inspiration, gives us the ability to operate in our area(s) of gifting with supernatural success. It is different than anything we normally encounter because it is a creative power, extending from the Creator Himself. It gives us a desire to inhale and exhale the Breath of God. That spiritual power carries with it a freshness that will revolutionize our call, our gifts, and our ministry. It is this second degree of the fire of God that brings illumination.

For example, many in ministry are serving within their call and operating within their gifts, but exhibit little or no creative power. This is because they've not "caught" God's fire—His imparted, inspirational, spiritual power. Power that is not inspired by God does not create. It is simply learned spiritual behavior. Creative power, on the other hand, will produce creative miracles, creative music, creative prayers, etc. Creative power changes people's hearts. It brings the fulfillment of prophecy to the forefront in God's timing. It is a power that is in perfect rhythm, timing, and sequence with God. And it is a power

God wishes to impart to His entire Church, particularly in the fullness of time of these last days. But we must be ready and willing to respond.

JUDGMENT IN THE FIRE OF ILLUMINATION

This fire of God represents divine judgment. By implication, it also represents discernment between good and evil. Before judgment can come, there must be a discernment of the good and evil involved. A judge in a court of law must have the ability to judge a matter by first discerning the situation, quite often in terms of good and evil.

This illuminating fire of God causes us to have supernatural discernment. In Joel 2:30-31, the prophet speaks of "the day of the Lord," when the sun shall be turned into darkness and the moon into blood. There will be wonders in heaven and on earth: blood, fire, and pillars of smoke. However, just preceding that reference, in verses 28-29, we read of an outpouring of God's Spirit "upon all flesh"; then, in verse 32, the Scripture declares that "whosoever shall call on the name of Lord shall be delivered [saved]." These Scriptures speak of a judgment of fire coming upon the earth, but the promise to the called and appointed of God is that this same divine fire will become a spiritual instrument of discernment. The Bible warns that in the last days there will be great deception that attempts to captivate even God's elect. (See Mark 13:22.) To avoid being deceived we will need to be able to discern peace, because First Thessalonians 5:3 tells us that when we hear the cry for peace, sudden destruction will come.

I believe that one of the biggest problems in the Church is lack of discernment. This spiritual lack has resulted in great leaders falling into sin and deception, the practicing of divination, New Age thinking and teaching, and moral sin being accepted rather than confronted—all among God's people. That's why the Breath of God, bringing illumination—hence, judgment and discernment—is so necessary for the Church today. And the important thing to remember about spiritual discernment is that it is much more important to be able to discern the move of God than it is to discern the move of the enemy, as God so graciously spoke to my heart when He said,

"For years now My Church has seen the works of My enemy, but they have missed the desire of My heart and the work of My hands. For you

have looked for evil in all your situations, but in these days you must learn to discern the good from the evil. If your eyes are focused on the evil, you will be incarcerated by darkness. But if you learn to respond to My goodness, My love, My works, you will be saturated with the light of My presence. I am calling My Church to a different degree of discernment. It is the judgment in the fire."

HIS PRESENCE IN THE FIRE OF ILLUMINATION

The other area that figuratively defines the fire of God is His presence. This term *presence* really means *before*. For instance, *before* the sun shows itself the sunlight appears. The presence of the Lord comes in as sunlight, and all who are there feel the heat and see the light. The manifest presence of the Lord is as the reality of the sunlight showing itself. It is not the same as seeing Him with our eyes.

When I wake up on a beautiful spring morning and step outside into the bright sunlight, I may not see the sun, but I feel its presence. The fire of God is as the Breath of God; the metaphor that best describes this is that I breathe Him in and am instantly, divinely influenced to produce for Him. I am enabled with spiritual power and the discernment to judge between good and evil. I have become a "package" with His presence.

As I said earlier, I have always been in love with God. However, it was not until a few years ago that I began to feel the reality of His presence. Now my prayer is that I will walk with an all-consuming, everlasting fire burning within and upon me, so that others will not only *see* Him but will actually *feel* Him. This is very important to me because I truly believe those in the Church who are not walking in the illumination of His fullness will not have the inspiration, the power, the judgment, or the presence they need to rise above the signs and trials of the times.

Please don't think I'm suggesting that I've arrived at this point. I certainly haven't, but I believe I'm on my way to understanding and flowing in this illumination and fullness because I have been "caught on fire" by the grace of the Breath of God, and that fire continues to burn within me. I did nothing special to make this happen; I simply *responded* to the Breath of God. Now I am inspired and empowered, and His divine discernment guides my every step, as I am saturated in

His presence. This presence within the fire illuminates us, and illumination is the first degree of the spirit of prophecy.

THE SPIRIT OF PROPHECY

One of the anointings of Ruach Ha Kodesh is the spirit of illumination and revelation. What exactly does this mean to us? A while back the Lord had me teach on the "Spirit of Prophecy and the Corporate Anointing on the Church." For about a year I taught and preached prophetic messages for the Church, all relating to these topics, and all before I had heard of the Hebrew term *Ruach Ha Kodesh*.

It all started as I was reading Revelation 19:10:

*And I fell at his feet to worship him. And he said unto me, See thou do it not: I am thy fellowservant, and of thy brethren that have the testimony of Jesus: worship God: for the testimony of Jesus is the **spirit of prophecy**."*

The concept of the "spirit of prophecy" so intrigued me that I began to study that entire chapter, which talks about the fall of Babylon and how that fall produced great rejoicing in Heaven. John the Beloved, who recorded the Book of Revelation as God revealed the message to him, was so overwhelmed with it that, when he saw an angel, he fell on his face and worshiped. The angel, however, immediately rebuked him, reminding him that angels are fellow servants of the people of God. (See Hebrews 1:14.) What the angel was trying to clarify to John also applies to us as we minister with one another: We must all work together in unity and have the same testimony.

Worshiping other people has been a real problem in the Church. Although there are offices and a leadership structure within the Church that we should respect and submit to, we have repeatedly seen the idolizing of spiritual leaders. Let me illustrate.

In the late 1980s I worked with Pat Robertson and traveled quite a bit on his behalf. There were times I purposely entered a place without identifying myself just to see how people would respond. In some cases, I received a sort of cold shoulder or a very aloof attitude—until I identified myself. Then everything changed. Even when people didn't agree with Pat on certain issues, there would be a change of attitude from the people present, and I would suddenly get a better seat. Pat would have been the first to object to such partiality. Due to my position of representing such a fine man of God, there was nothing wrong with getting a better seat, but there was something wrong with the spirit behind it. I should have been treated just as lovingly before I revealed my identity as after.

THIS MOMENT IN TIME

There is a testimony we all have, and that testimony is the spirit of prophecy. What is this spirit of prophecy? The anointing of the spirit of prophecy is a phenomenon that carries a distinction of beginning and end. Several times in the Book of Revelation our Lord calls Himself the Alpha and the Omega (the first and last letters of the Greek alphabet, meaning "the beginning and the end"). The angel told John that this spirit of prophecy is the testimony of Jesus, who is the Alpha and Omega. Naturally, since Jesus was, is, and is to come, and since He never changes (see Heb. 13:8), this anointing is indicative of time. For example, the anointing that comes in the gifts of the Spirit is an anointing that operates in the present for the present. (See First Corinthians 14.) The anointing to sing an already recorded Christian song affects the listeners *when it is sung*. The song, as well as the anointing upon it, may be beautiful, but it is limited to a particular *moment in time*. The spirit of prophecy differs in that it carries a *fullness of time* anointing that affects and encompasses all time at that moment.

Ruach Ha Kodesh contains not only the fullness of the Godhead, but also the fullness of time. Everything done under this anointing is released in this moment in time to reveal the One who was, who is, and who is to come, the Alpha and Omega, the beginning and the end. It is the reality of the past and present in light of the future.

The spirit of prophecy, which is our testimony, is the unveiling of Jesus to the world. Since the fall of mankind, there has been an anointing released to unveil the Christ, God's Messiah. Every individual who ever operated in the Breath of the fullness of the Godhead had a job to do, and that was to unveil Jesus Christ to the world. As we saw in Revelation, angels have the same job. They are co-workers and fellow servants with us. God's angels are active and working as a team with His Body, the Church. *The spirit of prophecy is the testimony of Jesus Christ.* Every member of God's army—whether angel or redeemed man—will ultimately give the same testimony.

Ruach Ha Kodesh, having all degrees of prophecy and containing the fullness of the Godhead, imparts to us a *knowing* (illumination), a *creating ability* (releasing of the illumination), and an *establishing* (doing/acting on the illumination). It is only through God's enabling grace, the anointing of Ruach Ha Kodesh, that this can be accomplished. Those who believe the gifts of the Spirit and the spirit of prophecy stopped with the Acts of the Apostles would probably disagree. However, I believe there are individuals today operating in this same anointing; furthermore, I believe that anointing is for the Church today.

The spirit of prophecy is life giving, like a "breath" of fresh air, replacing that which is stale or dead. It breathes life into everything, including the Law, because God's Spirit *contains the past,* but it *operates in the present to unfold future events.* Our Lord's voice remains a voice of today, not just yesterday. He did not die, come to life again, and then cease to communicate with us. He is alive, and His voice is alive, not only to address what has already happened, but also to speak to what is happening today and what will happen tomorrow.

Jesus is alive, and we do not exclude His voice because of faulty theology. To say that we can no longer hear the Christ is to deny that He is alive. Remember, Jesus came to *fulfill* (not abolish) the Law and the Prophets. (See Matthew 5:17.) It is in this moment in time that the spirit of prophecy is shaking the earth with tomorrow's reality: The Christ is coming again!

THE KNOWING PRESENCE (ILLUMINATION)

Have you ever met someone who possesses a unique quality of "presence"? I remember, in different circles of social exposure, there was always that one person who would walk into a room and command respect and portray a sense of authority. Others would almost be mesmerized by the person's presence.

The same is true in the Body of Christ. There are some who walk in spiritual illumination. When these people operate appropriately in this area, they carry a "presence" with them, which I call the "knowing presence" because these people seem to know something others don't. However, this presence is only evident to others when those carrying it are balanced and solid. If people will not submit to leadership, if they are emotional "basket cases" and/or are always having a "word" or a vision, if they always claim to have *the* answer (which is often nothing more than an opinion), then others will not recognize a "knowing presence" within them. We must be discerning about people who claim God's knowing presence while behaving in such an unbalanced manner, as they will often abuse the gifts of the Spirit and/or conjure up a message and label it a "Word from the Lord" when it is not.

In the ancient Hebrew culture there was a respect for the "knowing presence." There was even a certain protocol to follow when an elder prophet entered the room. People often found themselves awestruck in a prophet's presence. Our western mentality does not understand these things. And, again, we must never fall into the trap of worshiping mankind. But when I meet someone with a knowing presence, I recognize it, I respect it, and I want to be around that individual.

I can usually recognize someone with this sort of presence right away. People who have received revelation under the spirit of prophecy seem to "ooze" God's presence. Their eyes, even their mannerisms, show it. Everything about them says, "I know." And yet they walk in humility, confident that it is God—and not themselves—who has revealed such knowledge to them. Only maturity in Christ can bring them to that point.

To receive the spirit of illumination is to receive revelatory truths that begin with inspiration and move on to an empowerment for the Kingdom of God.

A Look at the Past

To better understand the following section, I strongly suggest you first read Proverbs 30:11-14, Matthew 17:17, and Luke 3:7.

Throughout the ages it has been difficult to trace the generations graced with Ruach Ha Kodesh. He was driven away by such sins as the shedding of innocent blood, idolatry, arrogance, and perversion. The Lord would then have to select individuals to "breathe" upon in order to call the corporate Body (people) of God back to faith. The

Jewish leaders say that Ruach Ha Kodesh abounded during the time of Elijah, who was known as the prophet of fire. Elijah first came on the scene in First Kings 17:1. In those days there was a school of the company of prophets. As a result, the spirit of prophecy was welcomed and sought after in their midst. In other eras of Ruach Ha Kodesh, the spirit of prophecy came upon individuals rather than groups, such as Moses, Deborah, David, and the major and minor prophets. This was due to the people's repeated cycle of sin (i.e., captivity, repentance, deliverance).

When God's people would backslide (fall into idolatry), they would find themselves in the hands of the enemy. Then the cry would begin for deliverance, and God would send them a deliverer. Immediately following, the people would be liberated from their captivity, but soon the sin cycle would begin again. History has proven that when sins are repeated over the course of generations, they become a culture and/or lifestyle. These cultures throughout the ages have bred a negative response and behavior toward the Holy Breath of God, driving Him away from entire generations.

In the past 25 years we have bred a culture that sheds innocent blood through the aborting of living souls. We have, for the most part, allowed and accepted it—in some cases, even practiced or participated in it. Some believe that certain pro-abortion groups, including many feminists, are working toward eliminating marriage altogether, blaming the covenant institution of marriage for violence against women and for trying to deprive women of their "right" to abortion. Some within the Church of England are attempting to abolish the phrase "living in sin" in order to stop condemning adultery. Other groups are trying to eliminate such words as wife, daughter, son, manhood, etc., all because they claim it is "extremely sexist." We have established a culture of rebellion, which the Bible declares is "as the sin of witchcraft" (1 Sam. 15:23).

GENERATIONAL CURSES

I was always taught that generational curses come through family lineage. Without excluding that reality, I would like to propose an additional thought about generational curses. Exodus 20:5 says, "Thou shalt not bow down thyself to them [graven images, false gods], nor serve them: for I the Lord thy God am a jealous God, visiting the iniquity of the fathers upon the children unto the third and fourth generation of them that hate Me." God refers to Himself as being a jealous God, punishing heirs for their ancestors' sins. This is a popular Scripture, used as a foundation in teaching on generational curses, and it speaks of both *lineage* (fathers to children) and third and fourth generations.

Now a generation is often thought to be 30-33 years in life span, although some believe it is 40 years. In studying this Scripture from a Hebrew perspective, however, we find that the Hebrew words meaning *third* and *fourth* were interpreted by the rabbis to mean "a process of improvement." The mind-set is that every generation should improve itself through *response* and *behavior*. Unfortunately, as stated in First Timothy 4:1-2, in the last days there will be a departing from the faith by those who will listen to and follow seducing spirits and doctrines of devils because their consciences will have been "seared with a hot iron." What inevitably happens to a generation of people is that, through their behavior, they pass along a culture to the next generation, which passes a culture on to the next, and so on. This is where we begin to find generational curses operating within a generation of people. The only way to break the ongoing cycle of these generational curses is through *repentance, response,* and *behavior*. This is called the "redemptive cycle." It does not exclude the process we find through lineage, but merely adds to it. One might say at this point that we are redeemed from the curse, and I would respond, "Yea and amen! *If* we continue in His statutes."

Sin that is bred through a generation affects that entire generation. Acts 2:39-40 declares, "For the promise is unto you, and to your children, and to all that are afar off, even as many as the Lord our God shall call. And with many other words did he testify and exhort, saying, Save yourselves from this untoward [warped, perverse, crooked, rebellious] generation." In contrast, Isaiah 44:3 and 59:21 speak of our offspring—future generations—being blessed by our covenant with Him. This is all designed for those who are "afar off" (our children's children) and are called of God. Acts 2:40 warn us to save ourselves from an "untoward" generation. This term meant that a particular generation was marked for destruction because of their rebellious response and behavior toward God.

God is raising up a generation that will respond to the Breath of God, a generation that, through appropriate response and behavior, will begin to cleanse an existing culture and people within the Church. The Church has been tainted by wrongful responses and compromised behavior. It has brought upon itself the curse of an untoward generation. The Lord redeemed us from the curse; however, we still have to deal with the consequences of our behavior. The Lord redeemed us from corporate humanity's fallen will, but we still have our own individual will to deal with. The message is loud and clear: *We must save ourselves from this untoward generation.*

The promise of freedom from generational curses is for us and for our children, *provided* we don't accept and practice the perverse ways of our culture but rather begin the process of improvement through proper response and behavior. This is how we and our loved ones will be set free from the sin cycle of a generation that has created a rebellious, God-rejecting culture. Jesus will return for a Church without spot or wrinkle (see Eph. 5:27), a people who will save themselves from this perverse culture. Ruach Ha Kodesh has been driven away for years because of a wicked and perverse generation. We mustn't allow that to continue.

If There Be Just One

In Genesis 18:23,25, we find the story of Abraham's intercession for his nephew Lot, as well as others within the condemned city of Sodom.

> *And Abraham drew near, and said, Wilt Thou also destroy the righteous with the wicked? ...That be far from Thee to do after this manner, to slay the righteous with the wicked: and that the righteous should be as the wicked, that be far from Thee: Shall not the Judge of all the earth do right?*

At this point, Abraham stepped into his new role as father of a multitude of nations. He felt compassion for the wicked as well as the righteous. Abraham's prayer is strategic. If there are just ten righteous within the city, then even the wicked should be saved. He was not just interceding for Lot, but for five cities that were condemned. (See Genesis 14:2; 18:26.)

In Jewish thought this is why Abraham began with 50 righteous (ten in each of the five cities). This was intercession for offspring and generations to come. The statement posed by Abraham is, "Be it far from You, Lord." How could God destroy the righteous with the wicked? What message would that transmit to other generations? Notice the focus. Notice the mind-set. How could their God inflict them with the same punishment as the wicked? Unfortunately, there was only one who was found righteous—Lot—and he and his family were saved.

A righteous person will stand publicly—alone, in "the midst of the city," if need be—with his God-given convictions. A righteous person— even if there be only one—will stand in the face of hostility. Abraham was graced with Ruach Ha Kodesh, and his intent was to breed a culture of holiness. His intercession was for the heathen as well as the righteous because he cared about the generations to come. The Breath of God lives in and imparts power to those who care about the generations to come.

While studying the spirit of prophecy I learned that there are 48 prophets and 7 prophetesses mentioned in the *Tanakh* (the First or Old Testament). There were many more graced with the gifts and office to prophesy. However, the reason these 55 were mentioned was because they impacted generations to come. It is very important to the Lord that we care about other generations and that we affect them with our repentance, response, and behavior (redemptive cycle). I believe that this generation God is raising up will be one that affects the present culture *and* the future, a generation that has the interest of those yet to come in their heart, because that is the attitude that reflects the heart of God.

A FAVORED GENERATION

For approximately two years now I have been preaching about a new and different generation, a generation not identified by age or human lineage, but by God's prophetic time clock. I have meditated extensively on First Peter 2:9, which speaks of a chosen generation, and have considered the meaning and import of the favor of God coming upon a generation. In John 20:21-22, the Lord breathed on a group of disciples before sending them forth: "Then said Jesus to them again, Peace be unto you: as My Father hath sent Me, even so send I you. And when He had said this, He breathed on them, and saith unto them, Receive ye the Holy Ghost."

Tracking this favored generation upon whom Jesus breathed, we find them in the Book of Acts, where Jesus gave them a mission, and with the mission, an instruction: "Go to Jerusalem and wait for the promise of the Father" (see Acts 1:4). In verses 6-7, the disciples asked Jesus about restoring the kingdom to Israel, but He explained to them that the timing of the restoration of God's Kingdom was not their concern. Rather, they were to be concerned with following His instructions so they could receive God's power and become His witnesses. In verses 10-11 two men dressed in white (angels, no doubt) referred to those who were with Jesus as "men of Galilee." This created a curiosity within me as to why, throughout the Lord's time here on earth, it was so important to allow the opportunity for future generations to recognize that God seemed to give favor to Galilee.

This was the time of the biblical Feast of *Shav'u-ot* (Pentecost), one of the three annual feasts to which all Jewish men, regardless of where they lived, were commanded to come to Jerusalem. The city was teeming with people, and yet Acts 1:15 specifically mentions 120 believers, including those who previously had been referred to by the angels as "men of Galilee." In Acts 2:1 we read that "the day of Pentecost was fully [finally] come," and the believers were "all with one accord [in unity] in one place." Then, as they waited, the fullness of God's time arrived. The promised Ruach Ha Kodesh came, and a new generation was birthed. This was the first time since the days of John the Baptist and his individual anointing (except for the Man Christ Jesus) when we see Ruach Ha Kodesh in the Second (New) Testament, the fullness of the Godhead coming upon them by the "sent" Holy Breath of God.

WHERE THEY WERE

Acts 2:2 tells us *how* the Ruach Ha Kodesh came, and *where*: "And suddenly there came a sound from Heaven as of a rushing mighty wind, and it filled all the house where they were sitting." The Breath of God came as "a rushing mighty wind." Where? To the place "where they [the believers] were." I believe it is important to understand that the Breath of God will come only where believers are present, as was the case in Acts 2. But what happened after that? "And there appeared unto them cloven [divided, split, parted] tongues like as of fire, and it sat upon each of them" (Acts 2:3). This was no accident. Keep in mind that this event took place on the day of *Shav'u-ot*, when the priests offered the first sheaves of the harvest on the altar, then awaited God's fire from Heaven to come down and consume the sheaves, signifying God's acceptance of the entire harvest to follow. Is it a mere coincidence that fire fell from Heaven and rested upon the early believers, signifying God's acceptance of them and all who would follow in their faith? I think not.

This was a prophetic, chosen generation, and they were right where they were supposed to be—where Jesus had told them to go and wait in order to receive God's power. Wherever believers go in response to God's directive, the Breath of God will meet them there. Then, because of their obedient response and behavior, they will have the ability to inhale His precious, Holy Breath. Others will savor their visits and their ministry. They will become an illuminated people, on fire with inspiration and creative power, piercing the darkness of the enemy and drawing others into His power and presence.

TONGUES OF FIRE

In John 1:32-33 a dove came upon the Lord Jesus Christ at His water baptism, and it remained there. This was God—Three in One—the Father sending His Spirit to rest upon His Son, the fullness of the Godhead. Then, in John 16:7, Jesus told the disciples that He must leave in order for the Breath of God—Ruach Ha Kodesh—to come upon them, another example of the Three in One.

The reality of the fullness of the Godhead is evidenced through the incident documented in Acts 2:2-4. The cloven tongues encompassed the entire Triune God—the Father and the Son, along with the Breath of the Spirit—thrust forth upon a highly favored generation. It came as fire, but it was the fullness of our Abba Father, the Ancient of Days. It was the Son of God, Lamb and Lion, and the power of the blood shed for mankind. It was the Holy, Sacred Breath of the two together. It came as a rushing mighty wind upon the place where they were, and they were filled as they responded and began to speak with other tongues. (See Acts 2:4.) Those who heard them were confused and asked in Acts 2:7, "Are not all these which speak Galilaeans?" Remember, the Breath of God came on a highly favored, chosen group of people from a specific geographical location, and it came suddenly where they were—and *only* where they were.

At that moment in time a new generation was birthed. At this moment in time a new generation is coming forth. This generation will be highly favored of God, and *where they are, He will be in His manifest reality.* There will be others around, but this will be a chosen generation, a generation graced with a Holy Blast of God's fullness!

THE PERFECT MATCH

Ephesians 5:26-27 speaks of God's desire for the condition of His Bride, the Church. He will sanctify and cleanse it with the "washing of water by the word" so that He can present it to Himself, a glorious Church, without spot or wrinkle. God wants to see His Church as it should be: holy and without blemish. Verse 32 then explains that everything we have just read is a great mystery because, although it is instructional for the marriage covenant here on earth, as God is concerned with marriages and families, the passage is really speaking of Christ and the Church. We must remember that Ephesians was written by the apostle Paul, and the doctrinal theme is based on the unity of the believers.

In preaching this message, I have often used the analogy of a single man looking for a wife. He sometimes looks for long periods of time because he knows exactly what he wants. In some cases a man can take one look at a woman, hear her express herself, and know without a shadow of a doubt that this is the "love of his life." He knows if this is the one he seeks. In other cases, he may meet someone and wonder if she could be the one, pursue her for a while, then, as a result of her response and behavior, know she is not. Sometimes the man will even go so far as to say, "That's too bad. She could have been the one if it were not for...."

The metaphor used in the Bible to teach us about our relationship to God is an illustration of our Lord Jesus Christ as our Bridegroom, with us (the Church) as His Bride. The Bridegroom will finally come for His Bride, and she will be without spot or wrinkle. The question is, How will He achieve this? The answer (simple yet complex): Through His Bride. The process? The local church. His earthly purpose? That they will impact the present culture and intercede for future generations.

The reality is this: Our Bridegroom is not coming back for a splintered, schizophrenic Bride. So how does He begin the process of bringing us to that place where we will finally be without spot or wrinkle? Remember, the Breath of God is thrust forth and sent. I believe that in these last days God is pursuing His Bride and releasing His Holy Breath upon her. He is searching for "perfect matches." I don't mean to imply that God is searching for perfect people, for that would be a never-ending, futile search; but perfect matches, meaning local churches that will receive His Breath. What does it mean to receive His Breath? Remember, Ruach Ha Kodesh (the Breath of God's fullness) has, throughout history, released His presence most powerfully during the times when an individual, a company of believers, and/or a generation did two things: 1) *responded* to Him and 2) *behaved* as He would have them do. Let's look a bit closer at these two points.

RESPONSE

Individual response probably is most important because this is what determines the rest—that is, the response of a church and a generation. (I should also mention that we are called upon to work out our own salvation with "fear and trembling." See Philippians 2:12.)

In my progressive travels, I have observed many things. When I first began in the ministry, in an effort to maintain a blameless walk I constantly found myself repenting because, when I saw something that "checked" me or made me uncomfortable, I felt compelled to repent for being critical. After some growth I realized that as "sent vessels" He sometimes shows us things so we can help others. (Why else would we be "sent"?) It was then that the Lord began to teach me to rightly discern (judge) the spirit behind my thoughts. When I was being critical, my assessment of another person's actions was saturated in carnality, especially when it involved something (seemingly) done against me.

A perfect example of this occurred while I was in India a few years ago. I was scheduled for nine crusades in a ten-day period, not to mention teaching at the Bible college in Madras. Pastor Sam Selva Raj, founder of Echo of His Call Bible College and Ministry and a dear friend, sometimes picked us up as early as 2:00 p.m. for a 7:00 p.m. crusade, even though it took no more than an hour or two to get to the crusade site. Because of jet lag and other challenges that are part of mission trips, I couldn't understand why he was picking us up so very early. After all, I was tired and had heavy ministry ahead. I would find myself saturated in carnality. At the end of our ten days, I found that it was all done strategically for a reason. There is much opposition in India to the gospel. The crusade officials were receiving daily threats and had to reroute us. What was for our good had become a fleshly struggle for me because I did not understand the plan.

However, when the Lord shows me something for the benefit of ministry, there is an entirely different spirit behind it, and I need not worry about repenting for my feelings because they are saturated in a sort of understanding compassion that causes me to give my all in order to meet the need for the hour. I find myself watching the whole encounter with the eyes of Jesus instead of with the foolish eyes of Irma. God has taught me to discern the feeling and attitude behind my own responses and behavior.

I also have observed many different responses and behaviors within the Church. The biggest culprit, I believe, is individuality. Individuality can be beautiful, as God created each of us individually and uniquely. However, it also can become detrimental, as a force that builds an invisible wall and keeps the Breath of God away.

Let me explain. Our Lord created the earth and the fullness of it. Every human being is His creation. When we become completely enamored with our own private world and individuality, how can we focus on His creation?

God is looking for those who, like Abraham, will intercede for individuals and nations. God's heart is reaching toward this generation and future generations to come. He is looking for those individuals whose identity is found in Christ Jesus, not in their own personal kingdom. Individuality, if not harnessed with the "Truth" (see Jn. 14:6), will breed a selfishness that neglects the things of God. We take our eyes off Him, as well as the present and future generations, and we end up focusing on ourselves. This is unhealthy individuality, and there is a lot of it in the Church. Unhealthy individuality is rooted in rebellion, and it finds its way into the worship team, the intercessors group, the secretarial staff, and even the pastoral staff. I have seen loyalty dismantled by "unhealthy individuality," a love for one's own world and identity. This is a carnal response to a Holy God.

For example, there are those who come to church but refuse to sing during worship. There are those who will not join in prayer or pay tithes. Others will not serve in any area of ministry, and some are in a constant state of agitation, caused by a judgmental, critical spirit. There is a self-absorbed idolatry within the Church that drives the Breath of God away and grieves the heart of the Father.

Imagine having a church congregation comprised of individuals with unhealthy individuality, breeding idolatry. Soon the church is full of people with unteachable spirits, religious spirits, Absalom personalities (usurping authority) in leadership, and Jezebel personalities (controlling, manipulating) in intercession. They may very well be saved and busy serving God, but their salvation and service is based on unhealthy individuality, causing a breakdown of vision within that local body of believers. How can self-absorbed people lay hold of a vision from God birthed by someone else?

The Breath of God is sent to local churches. The Spirit of God is omnipresent and, in His gracious mercy, remains with us as believers. But Ruach Ha Kodesh, the fullness of the Godhead, responds to hungry hearts. Of course, when the Breath of God is sent our way, there is always a response. The question is, *What will that response be?* God is seeking a perfect match. He is coming for a Bride without spot or wrinkle. As a Bridegroom knows His beloved, our God knows us. He knows our church; He knows our heart; and when He returns, we will stand naked before Him. When His Breath seeks us out, will our response be, "Here I am, Lord. What do You want me to do?"

BEHAVIOR

There is a saying within Jewish writings that reads, "Greater is he who is commanded and does, than he who is not commanded and does" (bt Kid 31a). This statement is tremendous food for thought. When the Lord gave the nation of Israel the Torah, He reminded them in Exodus 20:2 that He was their God, and He told them they must listen to Him. He also reminded them that it was He who had brought them out of Egypt, out of bondage and slavery. Then, in verse 20, Moses told the people not to fear because God had come to "prove" or test them, with the purpose being that they would not continue in sin. In verses 3-6 God commanded the Israelites to have no other gods besides Him, warning that if they did, it would adversely affect the generations to come. Ruach Ha Kodesh—the fullness of the Godhead, the Holy Blast of His Breath—was present on Mount Sinai that day.

When we are commanded by God to love, we must love, not because we feel it but because He commanded us to do so. "To obey is better than sacrifice" (1 Sam. 15:22). Jesus Himself said in Luke 6:27-34 that it is much easier to love someone who loves us than someone who hates us. And yet He commanded us in verse 27 to love our enemies. And so we love because we are commanded to love, not because we feel like it. Throughout the Scriptures God commands us to keep His statutes, live a holy life, and serve Him until Jesus returns. As surely as Ruach Ha Kodesh has been driven away in history because of wrong response, the Breath of God also has been driven away by wrong behavior. There are many in the Church offering "sacrifices," but God is looking for obedience, not just sacrifice. Local churches have developed a "sacrificial merit system" that has changed our focus from obedience to sacrifice through "busyness," and it has contributed to a culture that needs to be bathed in truth. It is our proper response and behavior that will draw God's Breath near.

THE SHEDDING OF INNOCENT BLOOD

When I think of the shedding of innocent blood, the first thing that comes to mind is violence, murder, and abortion. But there is another, less obvious aspect to the shedding of innocent blood that we, as the Church, have overlooked, and it has to do with response and behavior.

In the rabbinical teachings one of the sins mentioned that drives away the Breath of God is the shedding of innocent blood. To understand the value and power of blood we must look to the Levitical Law. Leviticus 17:11 teaches, "For the life of the flesh is in the blood: and I have given it to you upon the altar to make an atonement for your souls: for *it is the blood that maketh an atonement for the soul."*

The life-giving force within us is blood. Blood not only represents life, but it also gives life. Blood also represents the very essence of our being—where we came from, who we are, the nature within us, and everything we stand for. Blood represents every aspect of our lives as well as the life that created us. *Blood represents that which is behind us and that which lies in front of us.*

Most of us are familiar with the story of Cain and Abel in Genesis 4. Cain and Abel were two brothers, Abel being a shepherd and Cain a tiller of the soil. As with Cain and Abel, our occupations will always affect our methods of serving God. The difference in occupation and service between these two brothers led to jealousy and the first recorded incident of the shedding of innocent blood. (See Genesis 4:3-8.) Although there is much more to the story, it is important to note that it was jealousy that surfaced before innocent blood was shed. Cain was angry that his brother's offering was respected and received by the Lord and his was not. In his jealousy, Cain killed his brother.

The Lord then came to Cain and, in verse 9, asked, "Where is your brother?" Cain's response in that same verse was, "Am I my brother's keeper?" The Lord responded in verse 10 by saying, "The voice of thy brother's blood crieth unto Me from the ground." What Cain did not realize is that when he shed Abel's blood, his violent act was not limited to Abel's life; it also represented all of Abel's descendants. This act of jealousy had shed the blood of those yet to be born. When blood is shed, it is a sin against the Creator of life, the life itself, and lives yet to come. The Torah teaches us that this is a very serious sin and bears great consequences.

In Genesis 2:7 the Breath of Life was first imparted to man. That Breath carried within it the impartation of God's Spirit and blood, the blood of God that, as it coursed through man's veins, was contaminated by sin. Cain shed the blood that represented the Creator, the creation, and the fruit that would come forth from that creation. The Breath of God represents the blood, the life, the past, the present, the future, the voice of God, the power and the origin of all imparted to us. And so the "shedding of innocent blood" deserves and requires a closer look.

In Leviticus 19 we see a repetition of teachings in the Law. These teachings were viewed as revelation from God, and repetition was a method of impartation or learning. Leviticus 19:16 says, "Thou shalt not go up and down as a talebearer among thy people: neither shalt thou *stand against* the blood of thy neighbour: I am the Lord." Tale bearing and gossip are likened in this verse to bloodshed, also indicating that these sins actually can lead to bloodshed. If something that is said plants seeds of question and/or discord, if what is said can ruin an individual, we are coming against the Creator, the creation, and the fruit of that creation that is yet to come. Verse 17 then goes on to warn against holding hatred in our heart, the obvious command here being the very words of Jesus Himself: "Thou shalt love thy neighbour as thyself" (Mt. 19:19).

How often in my travels I have heard others shedding innocent blood with their mouths. How often I myself have been guilty of the same! This sin is said by the rabbis to be one of the primary reasons the Breath of God is driven away. I believe these sins of gossip and tale bearing have been one of the greatest hindrances in the Church to receiving the Breath of God. While we speak of evangelism and the transformation of cities, while we repent for the sins of abortion and violence, we overlook the sin of verbal bloodshed within our own camp and thus drive away Ruach Ha Kodesh.

Another teaching on this topic of the shedding of innocent blood is Ezekiel 22. Ezekiel was a priest and prophet who lived during the time when the nation of Judah was in captivity. Ezekiel received prophetic messages from God in the form of visions. In Ezekiel 22:9 the prophet reminded the people of the sin of shedding innocent blood. In verse 3 of that chapter, Ezekiel referred to the city that sheds blood, calling it in verse 2 a "bloody city." He told the Jewish people in verse 4 that they were guilty of bloodshed, but then he curiously moved on to verse 6, where he said, "Behold, the princes of Israel, every one were in thee to their power to shed blood." The word *princes* in Hebrew is *nasi*, which means, "Behold the Priest and the Prophets," the spiritual leadership of Israel. Verse 9 says, "In thee are men that carry tales to shed blood: and in thee they eat upon the mountains: in the midst of thee they commit lewdness."

Ezekiel was bringing forth a "missing link" for spiritual leaders, which is applicable to us today. How easy it is for a leader, burning in jealousy, to speak against another. James 3:12 describes this sort of sin as a fountain that continually yields both salt water and fresh, indicating that this should not be the case. Leaders today are shedding the blood not only of their peers but also of their sheep, as they carry tales from one church or camp meeting to another, or expose the confidences of others under the guise of "prayer requests." When the sheep cannot trust their pastors with personal information for fear of it being exposed to others, when one pastor is willing to put the reputation of another on the line because of his or her own insecurity or unresolved issues, there is no need for these leaders to pray and cry out for revival. It will not come until they first cry out in repentance for the verbal shedding of innocent blood. Leaders, through the verbal shedding of blood, have driven away the Breath of God from their lives and churches. As Cain was indeed responsible for Abel's welfare, we as leaders are responsible for the welfare of the Body of Christ.

In the Gospels we see that, before the blood of Jesus Christ was shed, there was a betrayal by one of those closest to Him, Judas Iscariot. But Matthew 26:59 tells of another betrayal of our Lord, this one by the chief priests and elders, the religious leaders of the day. Sound familiar? That betrayal came by way of their mouths, as they gave a "false witness" against Jesus in order to have Him put to death. Instead of responding in obedience and service to the very Son of God standing in their midst, these leaders responded by seeking His death! They wanted nothing to do with the Son of God. When we as leaders sin with our mouths, we are saying, in essence, that we want nothing to do with the Breath of God—and so we drive Him away.

The blood shed by our Lord was set in motion by the verbal sins of the priests and elders, as well as by Judas, who later said in Matthew 27:4, "I have sinned in that I have betrayed the innocent blood." In verse 24 of that same chapter, Pilate washed his hands before the multitude and said, "I am innocent of the blood [life] of this just person." The people then took on the responsibility as they decreed in verse 25, "His blood be on us, and on our children."

What does this tell us? The betrayal of life, the shedding of innocent blood, begins with the mouth. It is time to repent and to understand that, unless we respond and behave as God would have us do, we will not experience the fullness of Ruach Ha Kodesh. The Body of Christ, as a whole, has been as guilty of the shedding of blood as the murderer on the street or the abortionist in the clinic of the cities we are trying to evangelize.

THE BREATH AND GLORY OF GOD

In John 16:7, Jesus told His disciples, "It is expedient for you that I go away: for if I go not away, the Comforter will not come unto you; but if I depart, I will send Him unto you."

Jesus was saying it was good for Him to leave because He could then send His Spirit. John 20:21-22 says, "Then said Jesus to them again, Peace be unto you: as My Father hath sent Me, even so send I you. And when He had said this, He breathed on them, and saith unto them, Receive ye the Holy Ghost." Notice what Jesus is saying in these two passages of John. First, He says in 16:7 that He has to leave so He can come upon us in power through the Holy Spirit. Second, He would send His disciples forth as He had been sent forth by the Father. How did He send them? *He breathed on them.*

Jesus told His disciples that they would need the Holy Spirit to empower them. He also told them that they would be sent out even as He was sent. Then He breathed on them and told them to receive His Ruach Ha Kodesh—His Holy Breath. The key word here is *receive*, which means God's Spirit must be *fully accepted*. This means everything He is and everything He stands for. When I think of the Holy Spirit—about Jesus' warning in Matthew 12:31 against blaspheming God's Spirit, about the seven (or sevenfold) spirits of God mentioned in the Book of Revelation, about the day of Pentecost when God's Spirit came in power, about the warning in Acts 5:3 against lying to the Holy Spirit—it leaves me in absolute awe and reverence of Ruach Ha Kodesh. When I think about God and how I can trust Him, I realize I must have everything He will give me. And so I gladly open myself to receive the fullness of His Spirit.

Not long after Jesus breathed on His disciples in John 20, He instructed them to go to Jerusalem and *wait*. Wait, He was telling them, for the fullness of time. Wait until you receive power when the Sacred Breath comes upon you. At that moment they had a choice—either to receive and respond, or to reject and ignore. I believe this is what God desires now for His Church. When the Breath of God comes, there must be a response from the people of God. Once there is a lasting, consistent response from God's people, God will then respond with an outpouring of His glory, a glory that contains the manifest presence of His fullness.

If you are a pastor or ministry leader and have wondered why you have not tasted of this glory or presence of God, may I humbly and respectfully suggest that it may be because you have not responded to His Sacred Breath. If you have been desiring a personal fire in your life, think back on your response to His Breath.

Remember, God is looking for a perfect match, one who will respond to His Ruach Ha Kodesh. Jesus is coming back for a Bride without spot or wrinkle. As God finds these perfect matches throughout the earth, He will use them in the work of "spot removal" and "ironing" for His Bride. Although God is not a respecter of persons (see Acts 10:34), He is a respecter of response and behavior. Wherever that response and behavior is appropriate, God will pour out His Holy Breath on individuals and churches alike.

Like a husband-to-be, Jesus is seeking a Church that will prepare the way for His return. He is in pursuit of a divine romance with His beloved, and it is the Bridegroom's pursuit and the Bride's response and behavior that will remove the spots and wrinkles. There are wedding plans and preparations going on in Heaven, and everything will be just right when the fullness of God's time arrives: "Let us be glad and rejoice, and give honour to Him: for the marriage of the Lamb is come, and *His wife hath made herself ready*" (Rev. 19:7).

If you have been feeling the fire stirring within you, the urgency to "be holy," to be disciplined and pruned, you are a candidate for Ruach Ha Kodesh. Will you respond? Will you set aside your own vision and kingdom to build and fulfill His? Will you obey what He is asking you to do? Remember, sacrifice is not what He desires from you, but rather obedience, for *you will find your sacrifice within your obedience.*

THE DENOMINATION FACTOR

By now you may have concluded that I am of a "Pentecostal persuasion." However, when I speak of proper or appropriate response to the Breath of God, I am not referring to shouting and jumping. True, that may be part of our physical response to God's Spirit, but our primary response must be from our heart. We can jump and shout all we want, but if we don't first respond with our heart, the rest is futile and grievous to the heart of God.

While sponsoring a tour to the Holy Land, I scheduled a man named Joseph Baruch Shulam, a Messianic Jew who is the director of the Netivyah Ministry of Jerusalem, to address our group. One of his comments during his message shook me deeply, and I have never forgotten it. He said that the Messianic Jews do not want Americans proselytizing in Israel. "God forbid we should pick up their bad habits," he said. "We are Jews. We have the same Messiah Americans have, whether Methodist, Baptist, Presbyterians, Lutherans, Pentecostals, and so on. [But] we do not need [that sort of denominational] division; [we need] unity." He went on to say, "We are one in Yeshua."

I believe Ruach Ha Kodesh is for all true believers who are seeking God's holiness. And I am convinced that Christians from all denominations will have to make some serious decisions about His Holy Breath. We have entered a time when the hunger inside us, which has been placed there by God Himself, will take us beyond our theology and our opinions. If we are sensing this hunger, we are being pursued and graced with an invitation from Ruach Ha Kodesh to become a "perfect match." As we respond to that hunger, we will see God's glory rising upon His people, and others will see that glory in us.

God is gathering His people from every corner of the earth, a chosen generation, a holy nation, a match made in Heaven. Get ready! The pursuit is on, and when He finds you, He will surely breathe upon you the fullness of the Godhead, Ruach Ha Kodesh. May our prayer be,

"Breathe on me Your fullness, Lord!"

Chapter 2

TURNING THE WHEEL:
The Breath of God *Creating*

L et's give some thought to being able to *know* the heart of God for the moment, as well as having the distinct ability to *create* what He wants. What do I mean by this? A couple of years ago I did a teaching on "The Prophetic Word of God" and how, when the Word of God is released, it serves to *create*. Isaiah 55:11 says, "So shall My word be that goeth forth out of My mouth: it shall not return unto Me void, but it shall accomplish that which I please, and it shall prosper in the thing whereto I sent it." What is already *known* in the heart of God is transformed into a creative "unction" or anointing as God's Word goes forth, and it is then released into the atmosphere to "speak" something into the present in order to unfold the future. There is an authoritative anointing from God that actually *creates*, even as it releases the *knowing* in the heart of God. But in order for people to be used of God in this way, they must first take the time to *know* God's heart.

A simple example would be that of a chef who has the ability to create a beautiful meal but doesn't take the time to *know* the ingredients. As a result, the meal doesn't turn out as expected. We've all met believers who function much like that chef, haven't we? They sound anointed when they speak, but their *knowing* is off, so they aren't creating—meaning they aren't releasing anything creative from the Lord. They may speak a lot of words, but they don't produce any-thing. They are spiritually unproductive.

Isaiah 43 verses 1 and 7 says,

> *But now thus saith the Lord that* **created** *thee, O Jacob, and He that* **formed** *thee, O Israel, Fear not: for I have redeemed thee, I have called thee by thy name; thou art Mine....Even every one that is called by My name: for I have* **created** *him for My glory, I have* **formed** *him; yea, I have* **made** *him.*

These verses describe the process of creation within the prophet-ic realm. Notice the key words:

- created

- formed

- made

This is what I term the "turning of the wheel" by the Breath of God, the process of creation in the spiritual realm. The Lord created the universe by the power of His prophetic voice/breath. He teaches us that process throughout the Holy Scriptures as He creates, forms, and transforms. He *created* Jacob (meaning "the heel grabber"), *formed* him through a variety of challenges in his life, and *transformed* him, renaming him *Israel* (meaning "he shall rule as God"). (See Genesis 25–32.) The anointing of the spirit of prophecy is the very Breath of God released in the voice or spoken word. Once the anointing of the spirit of prophecy is released through the spoken word, God's "wheel of creation" begins to turn, forming and transforming.

For years there has been a lot of teaching on "watching your words" because by them we can be either snared or blessed. (See Proverbs 6:2.) Many reject this teaching, but God created the universe with His spoken Word, and since the fall of man the whole purpose of everything in His Word—and in ours—is to unveil/reveal Christ to the world. Remember what the angel told John in Revelation 19:10: "I am thy fellowservant, and of thy brethren that have the testimony of Jesus: worship God: for the testimony of Jesus is the spirit of prophe-cy." What the angel was saying to John was that angels and redeemed humanity have the same testimony, which is the spirit of prophecy. That's because, when we speak under God's anointing, our words carry weight.

To "testify" is to make a verbal declaration. Throughout history the prophets spoke and, through their verbal declaration, unveiled the coming Messiah. God desires to utilize His Church today to birth the fulfillment of prophecy. He wants to anoint His Church with the spirit of prophecy, the "testimony of Jesus." But He will do so only through those who can be trusted with the power of His anointing.

We must, therefore, be careful what we say, even as we are warned in Proverbs 6:2: "Thou art snared with the words of thy mouth, thou art taken with the words of thy mouth." What do we speak about ourselves, our church, our pastor, or those in authority over our government? How can God trust us with a creative anointing when our words are being used to bring destruction? When God can trust us with our mouth, He will trust us with His anointing. At the same time, let's bring balance to this thought. Not everyone is called to prophesy about future events. But whether we are called to prophesy or not, God wants all of us to *know* His heart for the hour in which He has called us to serve. This anointing, I believe, is an end-time release upon His Church to create and to set things in motion, which is the second degree of prophecy operating powerfully under Ruach Ha Kodesh.

Thus far, we have established that Ruach Ha Kodesh, the Breath of God, is a Holy Blast, releasing God's fullness. The fullness of His Breath contains all three degrees of prophecy, as well as the ability to operate in miracles, signs, and wonders. Those three degrees of prophecy are:

- illumination
- creation
- restoring/establishing

Within the first degree of prophecy—illumination—are the inspiration, judgment, and presence of Almighty God. Within the second degree—creation—is the creative power released by the Breath of God. Restoring/establishing, the third degree of prophecy, is the formation and transformation, or the finished product. In short, the Breath of God is sent to us that we may respond and obey. Remember, when Jesus breathed on His disciples and said to them in John 20:21b, "As My Father hath sent Me, even so send I you," the receiving of God's creative ability and anointing came to the disciples via His breath. When this happens in our lives, we have been graced to "set things in motion" in the present in order to unfold the future. When God breathes upon us, we have found favor and have been chosen. Can you imagine what could happen in a local church body if the Breath of God were loosed upon the people to turn the wheel that unfolds the Holy Scriptures to the world?

STEWARDS OF THE MYSTERIES OF GOD

Let a man so account of us, as of the ministers of Christ, and stewards of the mysteries of God. Moreover it is required in stewards, that a man be found faithful. But with me it is a very small thing that I should be judged of you, or of man's judgment: yea, I judge not mine own self. For I know nothing by myself; yet am I not hereby justified: but He that judgeth me is the Lord (1 Corinthians 4:1-4).

I will never forget, during one of my visits to Jerusalem, receiving a word from the Lord about revelation. It was close to midnight, and we were on our way to the Western Wall for a private tour of the Rabbi Tunnel. We had some time to spare so the group split up to spend some private time with the Lord. As we did so, I remember hearing the wind blowing softly and feeling the cold on my hands and face as I faced the wall. I looked up several times to gaze at a sky filled with the stars of the universe. Ah, Jerusalem, the jewel in His crown! What a joy it was to be there once again.

"Lord," I whispered, "I don't understand. Why me? Why have I had the privilege of making more than one pilgrimage?" I could almost feel His heart at that moment in time, a churning as if He were manifesting Himself within me, as He whispered to me in a still, small voice:

*"Dig deep, for there is much that has been fulfilled in Me that you do not even know about. This is the moment for you. Dig deeper and deeper, and you will find the fullness of the treasure I have for you. It hurts to see My Bride neglecting herself. It hurts to watch you defeated by the lies of My adversary. **Dig deep**! Everything has been fulfilled in Me. Not one jot or tittle of My Word should be ignored or denied.*

"I have called you to bring fullness," He continued. "Not just you, but others throughout the world." He then began to speak to me about including in my teaching the Jewish culture and the First (Old) Testament's meaning of Scripture. Finally, He said He was going to raise up people who would, by the Spirit of Revelation, tie the two testaments together.

The analogy God gave me at that time was that of a treasure chest filled to the brim with the riches of God. "*Dig deeper*," God urged. "*There is so much more available for you. Dig deeper and you will find the fullness. Do not stop at the halfway mark, but* **dig**!" He was stirring within me His longing for His Church to *really know* Him. Revelation comes only to those who dig.

I could almost feel an undefined impartation, or gift, from Him that night, a spirit of illumination. I was so inspired after that encounter I could hardly wait to get back home and apply whatever it was that God had deposited within me. I could "feel" the impartation, but I could not define it. All I knew was that I had to dig deeper!

That experience reminded me of Moses, who was given God's Torah (Law or teaching) on Mount Sinai. On that day God's chosen people, the Hebrews, were given "the Word of God." To the Jew, that is a day to be remembered and reverenced. The Torah was given to them and passed down to future generations, to be written on their hearts, taught to their children, and applied to their everyday lives. This was a day of great revelation for God's people. God Himself gave this command to care for generations to come. And for generations, because of God's directive, the primary focus of a serious Jew's life has been to study the Torah. In fact, for the Jew, there is no valid interpretation of life's issues apart from the Torah.

This divine directive to study God's Word continues to be a key attribute of a true man or woman of God. The Torah was given to the Jewish people for their time, but it also was given for future fulfillment. Through the years, God's prophets "turned the wheel" as the people of God dug deeper and deeper and found more of the reality of their future promise. We Christians must realize that Jesus of Nazareth, the Christ and Savior of the world, the One we worship and adore, was a Hebrew. He did not believe in man's ways, but He did believe in the Torah. He stood for everything in the Torah, and He did not transgress it at any point. When Jesus studied or taught from the

Scriptures, it was the Torah He read because the Gospels and epistles did not yet exist.

John 1:1 says, "In the beginning was the Word, and the Word was with God, and the Word was God." Jesus knew the Word because *He was the Word in the flesh*. It was through Him, the Living Word, that we received the Second (New) Testament, which gives life so abundantly. When Jesus Christ came into the world and became flesh (see Jn. 1:14), this became another Mount Sinai experience for His people. The Word, the great "I AM" (see Ex. 3:14), the "All in All," was given to His people. Just as that day on Mount Sinai, God's people would have to receive Him; this time, however, the Word was given in a different form. He who was, who is, and who is to come, *the fullness of God*, had arrived.

While the Israelites dug into God's Torah and found future promises, we dig today and find the fullness of all God's promises. As Christians we should not be fearful to look into the depth of *all* God's Word, which is *all of Him*. The two Testaments were made for each other. But the primarily Gentile Christians have been so cautious of the Law that many have thrown the baby out with the bath water.

Bible teachers have been careful not to bring in "too much of the Law," and those learning are taught to cautiously avoid it. Second Corinthians 3:6—"Who also hath made us able ministers of the new testament; not of the letter, but of the spirit: for the letter killeth, but the spirit giveth life"—is often used to justify this reaction. However, this verse is actually addressing the false teachers of that day who over-stressed the Law in order to keep the people in bondage. Those ministers who preach by the letter and not by the Spirit have a deadly effect on the people. When we preach and teach, we must do so with the fullness of God's Spirit. The leaders of that day were known for using the Torah to chain the people. To this day, any anointed, well-studied individual can get up and preach out of the Torah, with the Spirit of God upon it, and it will have powerful, positive effects on the people of God. The same minister can get up and preach from the letter of the Law with no Spirit and have a deadly effect that brings bondage. These religious legalists were utilizing the Holy Torah for leverage to control the people, and Jesus saw right through it.

The Hebrew culture has the most profound and rich customs in the world. I have found if we take the time to learn about that culture, we will better understand the Gospels and some of Jesus' actions while He was here on earth. The Lord's desire is to bring Jew and Gentile together in Him by the power of His blood. The message of His heart for us is unity. But before we can understand each other, we must learn about each other.

I once had occasion to get into a relatively deep conversation with a well-studied Jew in the Jewish Court. As I spoke to him and he responded, I was amazed at his understanding of Scripture. Only recently did I realize what it was about him that so impressed me. He was not Messianic, yet he knew more than most Christians about what the Gospels say and mean to us, simply because he was so well versed in the Torah.

I believe we have neglected to learn about the Torah, the House of David, the root and offspring of David. I am not suggesting that we neglect the Second (Old) Testament and concentrate only on the First; I am suggesting we stop neglecting the treasures in the First Covenant and teach the wholeness of God and the fullness of His promises to us. Through studying the two testaments, we will receive a divine revelation of the tapestry for eternal life.

THE MYSTERIES WITHIN

"It is required in stewards, that a man be found faithful" (1 Cor. 4:2). On that night in Jerusalem I felt an impartation, a divine gift that I couldn't define. I knew something had been imparted to me that gave me a sense of inspiration, but I couldn't put it into words.

Let's think this through together, shall we? All the mysteries of God are found in the Holy Scriptures. But where are they "housed"? If the Word became flesh and lived among us, as John 1:14 assures us; if that same Living Word—Jesus—gave His life so we could have life; if He is the revelation of the mystery of God, then within Him are contained *all* the mysteries and the fullness of the Godhead.

When I came to know Jesus as my Savior, I asked Him to come and live within me. The mysteries are found within Him, who is the Word, and the Word lives within me. This means that the mysteries are "housed" or stored in me, as He is in me and I in Him. I believe that as the Lord pursues us with His love, as He blows on us His Holy Breath, we are given an indefinable illumination. We can't easily or succinctly put it into words, but that's because *we must dig for the treasure* that is housed within us.

In the Jewish culture a religious Jew is called on to study the Torah daily. As a matter of fact, that daily study is considered worship to the Lord. Religious Jews hold the riches of the Word in great reverence, and it is part of their daily lives to read, study, and dig deeper. It is a *mitzvah* (command) from God to do so. The mind-set is to look into the Torah for the things of God because there is treasure hidden there. Every one of us who has called on the Name of Jesus Christ has the mysteries of God housed within us. The mysteries are found in the "letter" of God's Word, but they can come alive within us because God's Spirit is within us. According to First Corinthians 4:2, in order to be considered stewards, we must be found faithful. If we are not faithful, we will never dig through to the treasure of the mysteries in the Word hidden within us.

The promises at Mount Sinai were *future* promises for the First Testament heirs. As Second Testament heirs, we hold onto the *now* promises because all has been fulfilled in Christ Jesus—and He lives within us!

WHAT EXACTLY ARE WE STEWARDING?

Jesus said in Matthew 5:17-19,

Think not that I am come to destroy the law, or the prophets: I am not come to destroy, but to fulfil. For verily I say unto you, Till heaven and earth pass, one jot or one tittle shall in no wise pass from the law, till all be fulfilled. Whosoever therefore shall break one of these least commandments, and shall teach men so, he shall be called the least in the kingdom of heaven: but whosoever shall do and teach them, the same shall be called great in the kingdom of heaven.

Then, when Jesus was asked which was the greatest commandment in all the Law, He answered,

Thou shalt love the Lord thy God with all thy heart, and with all thy soul, and with all thy mind. This is the first and great commandment. And the second is like unto it, Thou shalt

*love thy neighbour as thyself. On these two commandments
hang all the law and the prophets* (Matthew 22:37-39).

Notice Jesus said the greatest commandments were commandments to love. Immediately following He stressed that the entire writings of the Law and Prophets were contained within these two
commandments.

Matthew 5 is, of course, part of the famous Sermon on the
Mount. Jesus was always being tested by His enemies, and when He
spoke those words in Matthew 5, He knew the skeptics were present.
So what did He do? He assured His listeners that He had come to
establish or fulfill—not abolish or destroy—the *Tanakh* (First Testament). He was telling them that what He stood for agreed exactly with
the Law (Torah) and the Prophets. These prophets had foretold His
coming, and now the Word had become flesh. The legalists, however,
could not—or would not—see it. The spirit of prophecy was *creating*
what the Torah had already *illuminated*, and the Word in flesh would
establish it. Here we see all three degrees of prophecy working
together.

Jesus affirmed His belief in the Law and the Prophets, and He
protested publicly anyone thinking for one moment that He would
seek to destroy those writings. In effect, He was saying,

> *"I do not relieve you, My Church, from your obligation to the precepts
> of My whole Word, but with My precepts I bring divine promises that
> set you free. Do not allow man to chain you with something created to
> set you free. The only thing I have come to destroy is satan!"*

If you look deep into the Word of God and biblical history, you
will find the anointing of the spirit of prophecy. If you study the pattern of Ruach Ha Kodesh within the pages, you will see that the times
He came most strongly upon His people were when all three degrees
of prophecy were in operation.

As stewards of the mysteries of God, we find ourselves operating
in the fullness of the anointing that comes with His Breath. Please
don't misunderstand me. I'm not saying everyone is a prophet; I am
saying that, as we receive illumination and revelation, we become
stewards of the prophecy. But we can't steward something we don't
have. What we are called to steward (care for, tend, nurture, cause to
be reproduced in others) is the revelation of God's mysteries. Where

do we find those mysteries? In the Word of God. Where does the Word live? Within us!

LEARNING TO STIR WHAT WE DIG UP

"Greater is *He that is in you*, than he that is in the world" (1 Jn. 4:4b). Did you catch that part? "He that is in you." Within you—and me—resides the reality of the Godhead. God's directive is to dig for the mysteries within us. But what's next? Once we've discovered those mysteries, what do we do with them? It has been my experience that, when we first receive a spiritual reality, we are on an all-time high. Unfortunately, because we're human, this high doesn't last very long, and soon we forget the height of our experience. I believe, just as people ritualistically visit the gym to improve their physical condition, we must visit the throne room and spend time with God in order to improve the stature of our spirit man.

Let me illustrate. I used to visit the gym an average of three times a week, as well as take a brisk walk every evening. I must admit, though, that in the beginning my exercise was simply an act of discipline. I seldom felt like leaving home, and I would usually arrive at the gym and have to push myself to begin stretching. But after I'd been at it for a few months, I began to see some results. Suddenly I didn't have to push myself anymore. In fact, I actually began to look forward to exercising, and I was concerned when had to I miss it. In other words, I "stirred myself up" to do something so I would look and feel better. Prior to that time I knew I needed to exercise, but I was not stirred or motivated to do anything about it. I had to get my will involved and discipline myself to do what I already knew I needed to do.

Things aren't much different spiritually. There are times when I begin to pray and I simply don't feel the anointing. At other times I simply feel too tired to pray, and it is a real struggle to get going and stay with it. But when I discipline myself to get started and to press through that feeling of weariness or lack of anointing, before long I begin to feel a stirring inside me. As that stirring grows, I become aware of a change within me—a powerful anointing and intimacy with God, rewarding results of disciplined prayer that cause me to *want* to pray, to look forward to my time of prayer, and to be deeply concerned when anything interrupts that time. This happens because

I have taken the revelation of the mysteries of prayer and "stirred them up." I am now *turning the wheel* that creates. I have been illuminated and greatly inspired. The "disciplined stir" creates a long-lasting effect that nothing can steal away or replace.

In these last days before the return of our Lord, we must know how to stir up the mysteries within us. If we don't, we will walk in defeat. Stirring up the mysteries of God within us takes discipline and obedience, but it will launch us into a victorious walk.

Spiritual Moodiness

I am certain that every reader has noticed the moodiness that exists in us saints from time to time. We might try to excuse it by saying, "Well, I'm only human," but moodiness derived from personal situations can be one of the most difficult feelings for any believer to encounter. I know because it has happened to me. I can be preparing to attend a church service, ready to receive, excited about being fed and inspired, and then suddenly run into "moodiness."

Moodiness affects each of us in different ways. Some people get sarcastic and say things that are uncalled for, or they may shun or hurt others. This is usually a result of unresolved issues in their private lives. There are other times when the seemingly strongest, most anointed people in the church become moody. There may not be anything wrong with their personal lives, but something may be off track spiritually. Although that "something" could be sin, that isn't always the case.

For instance, I don't consider myself a moody person. However, my ministry staff will confirm that I can become moody if something doesn't go right in ministry work. But there is something else that can really get to me, and I'm glad it does. It's when I feel spiritually "off" because of all the administrative work I must tend to, which can result in havoc within my area of spiritual responsibility. This sometimes creates a spiritual moodiness in me, both on and off the platform. I may feel the same spiritual power and effects, but there is something a little different in my delivery and ministry. Those closest to me can detect it, but I believe the general public can't. The work gets done, but I don't feel the same accomplishment afterward, and that bothers me. But I thank the Lord for spiritual moodiness because it keeps me "in check." It reminds me that I am moody because my spirit is grieved.

When we are on a spiritual high, we wish it could last forever. After all, a mystery has come alive in us, and we have been illuminated by God's Spirit. We are all held accountable for our knowledge or exposure to the things of God. Any time we have a spiritual responsibility and don't keep it, we inevitably become spiritually moody. I believe God designed it this way for our benefit and growth. When we are on a high, we are responsible to "stir the high" in order to maintain it.

When I am asked to minister at a prophetic conference and/or preach a series of revival services, I see the change in people. By the time we leave, they are on a high. Unfortunately, in most cases, they come down quickly because they don't keep that high stirred. The local church itself may experience a long-lasting increase, but the people didn't sustain their individual highs. If this situation lasts long enough, there will eventually be an undefined spiritual moodiness in every ministry and outreach of that church. Because of the power of spiritual impartation, I believe this spiritual moodiness can eventually be passed on to those in the congregation who are truly open to receiving everything their leadership has to offer. Soon they will feel the same spiritual frustration, as will the visitors, who, sensing an indefinable problem, will move on to seek another place of worship.

This brings a lack of fulfillment to individuals and to the local church. That lack of fulfillment, brought on by sustained spiritual moodiness, is one of the most harmful, ugly feelings in the atmosphere. The solution is in having the discipline to *stir*. We must *stir that which we have dug up.* This is why so many local churches have great meetings but can't seem to keep the fire burning. This is why we, as individuals, can experience the marvelous wonder of His touch and then feel a disappointment in the days thereafter. We need to aim at, not obtaining a momentary excitement that makes us want to shout and jump up and down, but a solid, stable high that keeps the fire going inside whether we're jumping around or not.

THE ABUNDANCE OF RAIN

Recently I preached on the "abundance of rain" mentioned in First Kings 18:41. It is the story of Elijah the prophet and his first prophecy. In First Kings 17:1, Elijah, at the instruction of the Lord, prophesied a coming drought. My immediate thought when I read this passage of Scripture was: *If one has the power to shut up Heaven with that which is within, then one also has the power to open up Heaven with that which is within.* This means Elijah housed the "abundance of rain" within him. It means that, through the bad and the good, he never stopped "hearing" the abundance within. Elijah housed the future—the mysteries of God—the promises and the inheritance. Even during the resulting famine, Elijah prophesied. He kept himself focused on God, despite the circumstances, because he could hear the abundance of rain. The answer was within him, just as it is within you and me. The King, the Master, the Lord of lords lives inside us! The rains don't begin when the Heavens open, but when we begin to turn the wheel of creation. The future lives inside us *now*. What Jesus Christ did for us was to fulfill what those on Mount Sinai awaited. The future has been fulfilled in Him. As we turn the wheel, we bring that future closer to its manifestation to the world. As a result, we become the testimony of Jesus Christ, as we operate in the spirit of prophecy.

Elijah was anointed by the Ruach Ha Kodesh. He was bold, and he was politically incorrect. His future and the future of a nation were living inside him, and he could "hear" it. There is something about spiritual hearing and seeing that we need to understand. Elijah told King Ahab in First Kings 18:41 that he heard the sound of "abundance of rain." When Jeremiah needed to hear from God, he was first directed in Jeremiah 18:2 to go to the potter's house in order to be illuminated with how the wheel of creation turns. Once he was illuminated, he received the message the Lord desired to relay through him—but first he had to *hear*. Elijah first *heard* the abundance of rain and was then determined to *see* what he had heard. Through God's instruction, the prophet "caught the vision" and *saw* a little cloud that soon translated into a wind and rainstorm. (See First Kings 18:44-45.)

If we dig, then we must stir. If we stir, then we will hear. If we hear, then we will see. And if we see, we will experience the fullness of God, for that fullness resides within us! There may be moments of dryness in us from time to time, but if we discipline ourselves to stir the riches of God, we will hear and, inevitably, we will see. But that creative wheel must be turned by us—His Body, His Church, His Bride—because that is our necessary response to Ruach Ha Kodesh.

Neither Male Nor Female

Galatians 3:28 says, "There is neither Jew nor Greek, there is neither bond nor free, there is neither male nor female: for ye are all one in Christ Jesus." I believe this is a topic that greatly affects the turning of the creative wheel. The gender issue in the Church has slowed down the process of the fulfillment of the prophetic wheel. We are His workmanship and creation, and when we don't function as planned, doesn't it follow that we affect the turning of the wheel?

I don't believe that God wanted to destroy the earth with a flood in Noah's days (see Gen. 5–8). Nor do I believe He wanted to come down and deal with the tower of Babel (see Gen. 11) or tempt the Israelites to build a golden calf in the desert (see Ex. 32). But all those situations affected God's creative wheel of progress. Could they have stopped what God was doing? Indeed not! But I do find it odd to think that some would propose that, after the creation in Genesis, the only ongoing creation is the procreation of living creatures. What about the unfolding of time and events and the fact that we humans are used of God as history makers? In addition, once redeemed by Jesus Christ, we become part of His Body. His Body is not dead, but very much alive. God accomplishes His mission on earth through Jew or Greek, bond or free, male or female.

I need to stop for a moment and point out that I have no personal ax to grind here because I have been very fortunate in this area. Since my days in politics, God has given me favor. God has surrounded me with people who don't seem to care about gender. The people God put me with always tried to help me advance, always attempted to pay me a better retainer, and always respected me as a lady.

When I entered full-time ministry, I could almost feel certain mind-sets thinking that I would minister to women only. Because I didn't know any better, I was satisfied with that; I love ministering to women. But, as is usually the case, God had a different plan from my own. Within months He had opened up the churches, and pastors were giving me their pulpit on Sunday mornings, as well as for days at a time. For some it was their first time having a woman in their pulpit. For me it was God fulfilling a desire of my heart that had not previously been voiced.

Galatians 3:28 tells us that there is no distinction in Christ. The apostle speaks of nations, social and economic conditions, and then gender, all being equal in Christ. There are two facets to our standing or position in Christ. The first is creative, and the second is redemptive. When we were created, we all were given our creative roles. Woman was given the honor of childbirth, the ability to nurture, and, as much as some women may not want to hear it, subordination in the union as a helper or partner for her husband. Man, on the other hand, was designated by God as leader of the union and provider of the home. These were assigned functions within the family unit, although both Adam and Eve were given dominion.

When sin came into the picture, it changed the status of our souls, but it did not change our God-given functions. Our roles remained the same. This affirms our humanity. In God's incredible plan to save our souls—not our functions—woman was used in her function to present redemption to the world. Immanuel ("God with us," the Son of God), born to a Jewish virgin named Mary, came into the world for the purpose of saving our souls, not our functions. It was from His shed blood that both male and female were redeemed, but the male and female functions remained the same. This principle applies to the family unit.

In looking at the second facet of our standing in Christ, the redemptive facet, we must answer the following questions: Could the blood of Jesus Christ be partial? Is it possible that the sacrifice and the power of the Lamb of God completely redeemed the male but not the female? Is it possible that our loving God sent His only begotten Son into the world to give males a new and better covenant, while not doing the same for females? Could it be that man is called to preach the gospel and make disciples, but woman is not?

The answer to those questions is found in our Scripture in Galatians, which tells us that, in Christ, we are neither Jew nor Greek, bond nor free, male nor female, but that we all have equal, inherent rights to the blood, the covenant, and the anointing of God—*all* the gifts and callings. The blood of Jesus Christ gives me my spiritual status. The promises of God are for "whosoever" calls on the Name of the Lord. Where the unchanged functions of male and female apply to the family, this facet of our standing in Christ applies to our souls being redeemed. The anointing, gifts, and callings are not partial to anyone. They are for the "whosoevers" of this world, male or female.

There is a rabbinical text that reads as follows: "I bring heaven and earth to witness that Ruach Ha Kodesh rests on a non-Jew as well as a Jew, upon a woman as well as a man, upon a maidservant as well as a manservant. All depends on the deeds of the individual." (Midrashic text: Tana Debe Eliyahu Rabba 9.) As the apostle Paul in his writing to the Galatians and this rabbinical writing show us, the Breath of God contains the fullness of the Godhead, and it is not partial to anyone.

Still, it is important to remember the difference between these two facets of our standing in Christ. Regarding the facet of function, the unit in the home remains the same. Men are to love their wives as Christ loves the Church, women are to respect their husbands, and both are to submit to one another in love. (See Ephesians 5:21,33.) This is the creative role for the family, an institution established and designed by God.

I once heard about a man who stood in the foyer of his church and told certain women if he thought they were inappropriately dressed. In some cases he made some of them cry. He really believed that, because he was a man, he had the right to comment on women's attire and even on how they served in the church. Although I believe both men and women can dress inappropriately for church, I also believe that this man was absolutely wrong in presuming to tell these women how to dress, how to serve, etc. Those issues are between the women, their husbands, and God—and, in extreme cases, with the leadership of the church. The point I am attempting to make here is that, within the family unit, there is an order; in women's gusto to answer their call to serve God, some have neglected their creative functions. At the same time, in man's zeal to keep his "post," he has often neglected the power of creation by hindering women from fulfilling their God-given callings. I believe this has been a major stumbling block within the operating of the church that grieves and drives away the Breath of God.

Both male and female have their distinct functions, which give them distinct personalities, which breed their behavior within their redemptive rights. This means we carry the personality of our functions into our work in the ministry. In our homes, our function is to be fruitful and multiply human seed. In our ministry, it is to be fruitful and multiply spiritual seed. These functions and personalities are what turn the prophetic wheel that creates and sets God's purposes and plans in motion.

I can't imagine what it would feel like to be told I could not preach or teach because I am a woman. I don't know what I would do if someone told me I could not have a ministry. What would I do with the messages God has given me? What would I do with the prophetic utterances? What would I do with the love I feel for God's people?

For years I felt content working in politics, but the day came when the Lord allowed me to feel unfulfilled. He knew it was time for me to move on. I began to feel a need to minister to God's people. I began to feel a wisdom in counsel that I had never noticed before. Since that day, all my passions and interests have changed. I couldn't bear to have those passions and interests taken away or stifled because that would be taking away my call and gifting, and it would strip me of my creative function.

Let me give you another example. I have three beautiful children, now young adults. Even in the toughest times I never felt unfulfilled in motherhood. It is a part of me, part of my calling and function. The passion for motherhood burns inside me. No matter how busy I become, being a mother is always a fulfilling delight and privilege for me.

I believe one of the main problems within the Church is that we don't understand these two facets or our standing in Christ. In the creative facet we have our functions as male or female. However, in the redemptive facet we have our gifts and callings for service in God's Kingdom. To be truly fulfilled, we need to operate properly in both facets. Many people are operating in their gifts and callings but not in their function, while others are operating in their function but not in their gifts and callings. As a result, they are out of balance and lacking in peace.

For example, suppose a man is called to full-time ministry. He operates with great power and anointing in his gifts and calling, but neglects his functions as father and husband. Or what about a woman who gets so involved with her domestic life that she fails to respond to God's call for service and ministry in an area outside her home? As men and women, we have been given our distinct functions; as redeemed humanity, we have been given our distinct gifts and callings.

Only within the institution of the family should our gender have any bearing on how we perform, for we are redeemed and anointed by God, whether male or female.

REDEEMED FROM THE CURSE

Have you ever thought about the curse God placed upon mankind in Genesis 3:16? "Unto the woman He said, I will greatly multiply thy sorrow and thy conception; in sorrow thou shalt bring forth children; and thy desire shall be to thy husband, and he shall rule over thee." In the next few verses God tells Adam that the ground is cursed, and by the sweat of his (Adam's) face, he shall work that ground in an effort to make it produce. Isn't it thought provoking to know that God cursed mankind in their function? God created us with certain traits. Woman feels the need to nurture and hold things together. She loves and loves to be loved. A man, on the other hand, feels an instinctive desire to provide. He loves being the protector and provider, and he adjusts very well to being served and pampered by his loved ones. So what about the "woman's libber" and the divorced man who abandons his responsibility? I believe they will never attain full, genuine happiness until they submit to their God-given functions.

We have been redeemed from the curse by the blood of the Lamb, but the functions for men and women remain the same. The way God creates, both physically and spiritually, is through our functions. The way the devil tries to destroy God's creative gifts within us is by crippling us, physically and spiritually, in our functions. The Breath of God gives us enabling grace in our function, physically and spiritually. By the blood of Jesus Christ we have been redeemed together, men and women equally, and the wheel must turn.

Men of God are called to operate within their physical and spiritual function. Their involvement in the Body of Christ is crucial. Women of God are also called to function physically and spiritually. This applies not only to the married couple, but also to those who are unmarried or who have had the unfortunate experience of divorce or the death of a spouse. Single people can serve together with the married members of the church to keep the creative wheel turning effectively.

TRAVAILING IN BIRTH

Galatians 4:19 reads, "My little children, of whom I travail in birth again until Christ be formed in you." Let's take the turning of the wheel one step further. Most of us have been taught that *travail* is in the form of prayer. And, although I agree, I must add another form of travail that accompanies prayer. I have heard people say, "You can't just pray and forget it; you must pray and press in." In other words, *do* something. There is truth to this advice, although I'm not talking about *making* things happen, for that only creates more problems. When I talk about doing something, I'm referring here to our function. When the Breath of God, Ruach Ha Kodesh, comes upon us, He enables us and expects us to respond *in our function.*

We cannot deny our Creator; we cannot stop at salvation. We must go on to maturity, and that means learning to serve within our God-given function. As the people of God learn to step into their functions within their homes, churches, and ministries, the creative wheel will turn properly. Then, as the wheel turns, we will be used by God to create, give birth, provide, and nurture; and as we serve in this capacity, Christ is formed in us and in others.

There is neither male nor female in Christ Jesus. In Christ there is equality; in the blood of Jesus there is restoration for both male and female. If a woman feels the Word of God burning in her like a fire, if she feels the power of God flowing through her fingers, she needs to respond, regardless of her gender. When we don't respond to God's call on our lives, we drive away the Breath of God. We can't allow mankind's doctrines to hold us back from serving God. We all have been redeemed by the blood of Jesus, and the anointing is for all of us, male or female. No one can rightfully deny the anointing and calling of God.

GOD'S ANOINTING

As always, I will attempt to bring balance to my comments. According to Ephesians 4:7, we are given a "measure" of God's anointing. There are "office anointings" and "gift anointings," or different levels of anointing—all of which are powerful. There is a difference and a distinction, however, between the power that is released through ministers who operate in the "office anointings" and the power that is released through individuals who operate in "gift anointings." But one thing is the same, and that is the anointing in and of itself. It may be given by different measures, but it is given by the same Spirit. In other words, the anointing is neither male nor female because God is Spirit, and this anointing is released with no gender identification or preference.

When I minister from the platform, I observe many different types of listeners in the audience. In addition to those who come to receive from God, some come merely as spectators, to observe and confirm themselves, while others come as critics, to critique the minister and all that takes place at the meeting. These spectators and critics hear the message but do so with ulterior motives. Because of the carnal spirit behind their motives, they look at the minister through natural rather than spiritual eyes. Maybe they will like the minister; maybe they won't. Maybe they will like the delivery; maybe they won't. Of course, everyone is entitled to his or her own opinion, but there are two areas no one is entitled to except God, and that is in judging the heart of mankind and in judging the heart of the Spirit. When we pass judgment on the heart of the minister carrying the anointing, we grieve the One who bestowed that anointing. When we judge God's Spirit, we drive Him away. Both are ugly, serious offenses to God.

Many people try to figure out why God bestows greater measures of anointing on some than others. The fact is, God is not a respecter of persons, as we see in Acts 10:34, nor does He look at gender. Instead, He looks at the heart. God is not concerned with whether we dress in the latest styles or wear the right hairdos or drive the best cars, although some people consider such things important. How foolish! What do the Scriptures tell us about the Kingdom of Heaven? According to Matthew 19:14, it is made up of those whose hearts are childlike. Children approach the Spirit of God simply, blinded to trends and philosophies. We must learn to do the same, for God anoints His Church, male or female, rich or poor, according to *His* measure, not ours. When we learn to do that, we will begin to operate in the fullness of the Godhead, Ruach Ha Kodesh.

THE PROPHETIC WOMB OF THE NEW MILLENNIUM

Those who have experience in intercession and/or motherhood understand the term *travail* only too well. It is otherwise known as "the labor of childbirth." Travailing is not pleasant, but it is necessary in the birthing process. Romans 8:22 says, "For we know that the whole creation groaneth and travaileth in pain together until now." Even God's entire creation experiences the sometimes agonizing process of travail. Throughout the Bible there are several Scriptures that refer to spiritual travail and others to natural travail. For our purposes, we will focus on spiritual travail.

As believers we have been impregnated with the promises of God. Once we stir those promises up, once we "hear" the abundance of rain as the prophet Elijah did, then we want to "see" the fulfillment of what we have heard and felt within us. But it takes a process of travail to get to that point. That travail, sometimes easier than at other times, may occur through our prayer or through our function. This process of travail is what effectively turns the wheel. But where there is travail, there must also be a "womb." Where, in this spiritual travail, is the womb?

Proverbs 4:23 warns, "Keep thy heart with all diligence; for out of it are the issues of life." We don't keep things in our will or in our emotions, but in our heart. The spiritual womb is the heart. I am impregnated with the promises of God. Mary, the mother of Jesus, kept the things pertaining to the promises of God in her heart. (See Luke 2:51.)

Earlier I shared with you the three degrees of the spirit of prophecy, which are released by Ruach Ha Kodesh. Creation is the second degree, which I've been addressing in this chapter. We have seen that, first, we are illuminated by God's Spirit, and then we begin to turn the creative wheel with our travail. Until recently, we have been such a spoiled people that we have focused only on our own hearts. This is evident in our prayer time—the way we begin, the way we pray, and the way we close with the Lord. All is focused on us rather than on Him and the desires of His heart. To God, our heart is important; He cares about our every need. But what about God's heart?

We are the Body of Christ—this means *all* true believers, not just Baptist, not just Pentecostals, not just Messianic Jews. Something began to stir in the Body of Christ recently, and it is a revelation of unity. For years we have talked about it, but it is not until a revelation hits the corporate Body that preachers and pastors begin to teach on it. Unity has become a fresh topic. This is because God wants us to focus on His heart, the prophetic womb of the new millennium. If we are His corporate Body, then we have one womb as a Church, and that womb is the heart of God. How can we know the heart of God if we, as His people, are not in unity? The heart of God is in His Body, the Church. A scattered, fragmented Body will not receive the fullness of revelation. The whole creation groans and travails in pain *together*, remember? But as God's people travail in prayer, what are they birthing—that which is in their own hearts, or that which is in God's heart?

The heart of God is impregnated with all the souls of the world. He is concerned not with one marriage, but with all marriages; not with one abused child, but with all abused children; not with one drug addict, but with all drug addicts; not with one local church, but with all local churches. It's time for unselfish travail and birthing. Those attempting to build their own kingdom, who don't care for other ministries and churches, are not hearing the heart of God. We have been a selfish people, focused on our own womb, travailing to bring forth our own visions and desires.

Those of us who know and love Jesus need to come together as one to travail and birth the heart of God. As we do, we will be loosed from bondage to self and will begin to travail as a corporate Body. If we want to see a move of God in our midst, if we want to see miracles and be involved in building the Kingdom of God, then travailing in unity to birth what is in the heart of God is a must! God is holding the promises of the end-time harvest. He is holding the reality of revival, miracles, signs, and wonders. They are all housed in the prophetic womb of the new millennium. Christ is the Head, we are His Body, and His heart beats within us.

The Lord has shown me that we will not see His fullness until we come together to travail in unity, and that unified travailing will begin in our local churches. It is the hour for Ruach Ha Kodesh to come upon the Church in fullness. The greater works Jesus spoke about are not coming upon a fragmented, schizoid Church bound by pride, envy, and competition. When is the last time we prayed for someone else's church, someone else's ministry? When is the last time we asked God to anoint the other singer scheduled for the same function? Our focus must change. We are to continue to pray for the things God has given us and asked us to steward, but we must learn to *hear* and respond to the heart of God, and then we will see the greater works.

I believe this to be the ultimate increase within the second degree of the spirit of prophecy. Once a church or city is illuminated with this reality and stirs it up, the turning of the creative wheel will increase in speed. The prophetic womb of the new millennium is yearning for God's Body to line up with His heart.

Chapter 3

BEARING FRUIT THAT REMAINS: The Breath of God *Establishing* and *Restoring*

We now come to the third degree of the spirit of prophecy. In John 15:16 Jesus said, "Ye have not chosen Me, but I have chosen you, and ordained you, that ye should go and bring forth fruit, and that your fruit should remain: that whatsoever ye shall ask of the Father in My name, He may give it you." Being chosen is directly related to bearing fruit—not short-term fruit that rots and falls off the tree, but fruit that remains.

There are two areas related to bearing lasting fruit that I would like to address: *establishing* and *restoring*. Through the numerous messages I have prepared on the prophetic and apostolic anointings, I have found that establishing and restoring work hand in hand. The prophetic sets things in motion, and the apostolic establishes that which has been released. Therefore, let's look first at establishing.

ESTABLISHING

When a prophetic ministry is invited and/or sent to a local church, it is a ministry assignment focused on setting something in motion (i.e., illuminating, turning the wheel, and establishing). What some do not realize is that the prophetic impartation or gifting is bestowed on a church according to the *measure* in which the people receive it. This means the work can be stifled by the rejection of the gifting/anointing.

I have noticed two situations that seem to be very common in stifling the prophetic impartation, and neither involves overt sin. One is when the people really want a particular minister to come to their church, but the pastor doesn't. The people push and nudge until they finally get their way. The minister arrives and immediately feels the coolness from the pastor and his wife, as well as the suffocation of the anointing. It practically ties the visiting minister's hands.

The other situation I see quite often is when the pastor/leadership desires a powerful, refreshing move of God, but the people don't. The congregation, for the most part, is satisfied with the status quo and doesn't want to rock the boat. You've heard of "squeaky wheels," haven't you? I'm not necessarily referring to the whole church, just a group that "squeaks" when the creative wheel is turned. (Those squeaky wheels can even be within leadership.) Because of the noise these squeaky wheels make, people put up with them and sometimes even join them. But that squeaking noise is the sound of rebellion, which, according to First Samuel 15:23, is "as the sin of witchcraft." My heart goes out to churches like that because, unless the problem is corrected, they will never see the move of God in fullness.

Again, to bring balance to this statement, I'm not saying God's Spirit leaves that church. I am saying the Breath of God, Ruach Ha Kodesh, is driven away. If we truly want to see a powerful move of God in our churches, families, and cities, whether we are members of the clergy or the congregation, we must stop being squeaky wheels, lay aside the building of our own kingdoms, and open ourselves to what God wants to do in our midst.

As a prophetic minister I have personally experienced these types of incidents, and it is a very unpleasant time for my ministry team and me. The anointing is stifled. God still moves because He is faithful, but the move is not in fullness. The problem is, when there is "division in vision," how can anything set in motion be established?

We have addressed the illumination brought about by Ruach Ha Kodesh. We have looked at the turning of the wheel, which is needed to set things in motion as the Breath of God is released in fullness.

Now we look at establishing. When we establish that which God has set in motion, we begin to see fruit that remains. The prophetic deposit begins a work in the Spirit and sets things in motion for the church or city. Pastors will often call on outside speakers to impart a fresh touch, bring a prophetic message, or stir the gifts. Then comes the establishing.

THE PROGRESSIVE MOVE

Over the years I have observed the progressive move within impartations, or giftings from God. I learned to recognize the distinction of the office anointing from the gift anointing. I began to comprehend the reality of the measures of anointing. When I come into a church, the first thing I do is focus on the three degrees of anointing from Ruach Ha Kodesh—illumination, creation/turning the wheel, and establishing/restoring. When I am able, I work my way through all three in my teaching, in order to help the people better understand the degrees of prophecy. Unfortunately, I'm not always able to do that because of the lack of receptivity of the people and/or sin in the congregation (or staff). In some cases, the pastor will schedule us to come back before we even leave, sensing that there is "unfinished business." I've also had pastors meet with me when our time together is finished to ask for input and counsel concerning their undefined feelings.

In order to set something in motion, those being called upon to turn the wheel must first receive what God has for them. When I can get to the third degree of the anointing in a church, I recognize the apostolic impartation—the gifting that allows the "new thing" from God to be established. Those gifted in even elementary discernment feel a great excitement as they witness the turning of the wheel for their church. It is exciting to watch the anointing reach this level because this is where we see action put to illumination and hands to the wheel. It is gratifying to minister in a church and see the people move into this area of ministry.

Last year the Lord spoke to me about two small towns in California—Merced and Lodi. In January 1999 I co-sponsored a prophetic conference on the blood of Jesus Christ with a good friend of mine, Pastor Randy Bissell. The event was held at his church, Christian Life Center in Merced. It so happens that Merced (which, by the way, is Spanish for "mercy") is situated smack dab in the center of California. As a result, someone called it the "mercy seat" of California.

As we ministered throughout the conference, we focused on the blood of Jesus Christ. The first night we "launched" the weekend by taking communion together. On another night we had many pastors in attendance, and the Lord prompted me to call them to the front to join with us to repent for the sins of the State of California. During that conference I felt the first degree of prophecy being released, but I sensed the ministry time would need to be repeated on a strategic timetable in order to see the second and third degrees of prophecy released in that church as well. Sometimes the progressive work comes in one meeting, but often it takes several meetings to work through all three degrees of prophecy.

In Lodi, California, the Lord gave me a prophetic message for the city. The message was "Talitha cumi, Lodi" ("Lodi, arise.") From that message, a mission was given to me to focus on illumination. I know I'm not the answer—God is—but I must do my part. God showed me the only obstacles to receiving His Breath in Lodi were the people of Lodi. I began my ministry time there by holding some very powerful meetings, and I soon recognized a great need for prayer. I sensed God saying that if they would make prayer their focus, He would release His anointing in His time. A local body of believers must be open to being illuminated. If they're not, they will have meeting after meeting, possibly experiencing God's grace and power for the moment, but nothing lasting—fruit that remains—will be established.

Many don't understand this and question the effectiveness of the minister or ministry/church, all the while rejecting the very gift sent by the Breath of God. When we attend a church service with the intention of proving ourselves right and the pastor or minister wrong, we are grieving the Holy Spirit of God. Ruach Ha Kodesh doesn't come simply to inspire us or to create a stir. The Lord desires to *establish* His work.

For those of you who are familiar with the Brownsville revival, I can assure you that all three degrees of the spirit of prophecy were in operation there. Soon after the revival began, the leaders sought to establish what God had released, operating in an apostolic anointing. They wrote books and held conferences in an attempt to encourage and train others. Prayer continued unabated, and God's Spirit moved in fullness because the work was being established.

I have been in meetings where the power of God moved but no lasting fruit was established. Sometimes it was because of division in spiritual leadership. At other times it was due to immorality or disloyalty within the church family. As a result, although God desired to pour out His fullness, the people didn't respond. But the Breath of God continues to seek a place where the people are hungry, where they will put aside their own agendas and respond to Ruach Ha Kodesh so that His work may be established on the earth.

RESTORING
The Progressive Growth of the Prophetic Seed

Moving from establishing to restoring, let me first give my definition of the word. To *restore* might be described as a sort of rebuilding, but in the context of the third degree of prophecy, the meaning is closer to "reestablish." When something is established, it becomes permanent—settled once and for all. When something needs to be reestablished, it isn't because it was never established. Rather it was neglected and forgotten, or possibly that which had been established was tampered with and stripped of its definition, existence, and value.

There are certain things that have been established on earth as in Heaven, such as the will of God, the purpose of God, the plan of God, and the power in the blood of Christ. In Matthew 6:10, part of what is commonly called the "Lord's Prayer," are the words, "Thy kingdom come. Thy will be done in earth, as it is in heaven." That which has been established remains here on earth, even as it does in Heaven. I believe that, somewhere along the line, God's adversary, the devil, began to tamper with that which had been established. He hasn't been able to destroy what God established, but he has tampered with it in an attempt to strip it of all dignity and definition. And that's why we now look at reestablishing, or "restoring to its original state" what God has previously established.

Ruach Ha Kodesh (the fullness of the Godhead) contains the Father, Son, and Holy Spirit. When His Breath comes upon us, it is an attempt to impart God's fullness. Within that fullness are all three degrees of prophecy and all three degrees of the anointing of the spirit of prophecy (illumination, creation, and restoring/establishing). To arrive at the third degree is a step in maturity for any individual who walks with the Lord. But it also can apply to a word that has been prophesied. Did you know that a prophetic word matures in the Spirit? It grows like a seed. These three degrees are what bring fulfillment to the word that has been released. This is precisely why many walk around with unfulfilled words: They stopped at the first degree. They were illuminated but moved no further. But when an individual or a prophetic word of God reaches the third degree of prophecy, we are ready to see the bearing of "fruit that remains." What do we really mean by that term?

Fruit that remains is long lasting. It is fruit that has been established. In other words, it will not rot with time or season. Once that fruit is brought forth, it remains. When I think of it in these terms, I come to the conclusion that I'm far from satisfied with my own crop. In retrospect, I still have a lot of work to do. First, there are things I must *establish* by faith; second, there are things I must *reestablish* by faith. When we talk about the hour of restoration, we are talking about the hour of *reestablishing*. In Joel 2:23, the prophet began to encourage God's people as he spoke of bringing "former" and "latter rain." Immediately following in verse 24, Joel spoke of increase. And in verse 25 he told the people that God would restore—reestablish—the years that were eaten up.

In this passage from Joel we see the third degree of the spirit of prophecy. Rain illuminates, increase comes through turning the wheel, and restoration comes through reestablishing something seemingly no longer established. Joel went on to say that everyone would know that God was in the midst of His people. He also promised that God's people would never be ashamed. While studying the Major and Minor Prophets, I saw the progressive growth of the prophetic seed, which always serves to establish and reestablish, bringing forth fruit that remains.

HALAKHAH: THE PATHWAY TO HOLINESS

In John 14:6 Jesus said, "I am the *way*, the truth, and the life." There is a *way* we should walk, a sort of "holy highway." When John the Baptist came, it was to prepare the *way*. Before we can get to the truth and life of John 14:6, we must get on the *way*, the right path.

Jesus didn't say, "I am one of many ways." He said, "I am *the way*," meaning the *only way*. Throughout the Torah, God instructs His people to *walk* after God. This really means to walk after His presence, which can be found only when we walk on the correct path, in *the way*. The early believers in Jesus, before they were ever referred to as Christians, were called "followers of *the way*."

In the Second Testament, it tells us in First John 4:4 that "greater is He that is in you, than he that is in the world." In Romans 8:11 the apostle wrote that the same Spirit who raised Jesus from the dead resides in us. Jesus said He is *the way*. Why did He have to come into us? Why couldn't He just lead us? The answer is that we are His Body. Where else would He live? Jesus Christ came to take up residence within us so He could take us home. The way home, the way to God, is in us! Therefore, His presence is in us and around us. We don't need a cloud by day or a pillar by night. (See Exodus 13.) The day we called on Jesus Christ was the day the *way* came into us to show us the way home. There is a difference between finding the right road or path—the way—and then sitting down on the side of that road to wait, and finding the right road or path—the way—and walking along or after it. In other words, it's not enough to have the revelation of "occupancy"; there must be corresponding action.

This is what I enjoy so much about the Hebrew thought on Scripture. The apostle Paul said throughout the epistles that we have not been saved by our works—and, indeed, we have not. Eternal life comes by grace and is a free gift from God. (See Ephesians 2:8-9.) In James 2:17 we see that faith without works is dead. James goes on to say in verse 18 that he will exhibit or prove his faith by his works. Once we're saved, there must be corresponding action to show our faith. There is a common but mistaken belief in some Christian circles that, once we're saved, all we have to do is feed ourselves spiritually and be good witnesses. Although those things are important, this is far from the complete truth. God doesn't want us to be defeated in our earthly lives. True, it is the ultimate wonder to obtain eternal life, but God wants us to live victoriously, even while we are here on earth. How do we do that? We do it by faith, for genuine faith is what motivates and spurs us to godly works.

In Genesis 17:1 the Lord told Abram to *walk before Him* and be "perfect." The word *before* in this context means to walk "sooner" than, or in front of. "Become close to Me through your efforts," God was saying, "and it will breed perfection." Some question the ability to walk right and be perfect. However, this is the process of *walking in the way*. It is not being perfect in and of ourselves, for we know we will not reach perfection until we are in our eternal home. It is moving toward perfection through our efforts. The condition of our walk with God on this earth is established in our efforts. Without effort there is no real or saving faith.

We know that God goes before us, walks with us, and is in us. (See Leviticus 26:11-13.) However, to step out in faith is to step out *before* Him. In Numbers 32, we read about the Reubenites and Gadites, two of the tribes that approached Moses and, because of their cattle, asked if they could stay on the east bank of the Jordan rather than cross over with the other tribes. Moses couldn't believe they didn't want to cross over into the Promised Land (the west bank) or that they would allow their brothers to go to war while they sat and watched. Even the Lord was angry with them. God had told them to *cross*, to *walk*, and to *conquer*, but they wanted to stay in the comfort zone.

Believe it or not, the desert was tough, but it was in the desert that the Israelites had every need met without any effort on their part. God wanted to give them the Promised Land, but in order to receive it they were being called by God to *cross* (step out), *walk* (take the land), and *conquer* (fight for it). They were being called to take a "leap of faith," to step out *before* God simply because He told them to. They had lived effortlessly in the desert as all their physical needs were met; now it was time to grow up.

How can we expect to see the "greater works" Jesus spoke of in John 14:12 without first exercising our faith? And how do we have faith without works? Very simply, we don't. When God calls us to take a leap of faith, we need to step out—even if it seems we are stepping out ahead of Him—and move forward in faith, for without faith it is impossible to please God. (See Hebrews 11:6.) There is a way we should walk, and it is based on the framework of the Ten Commandments, with "Thou shalt" and "Thou shalt not" as the electrifying motivation. Those who walk accordingly will find themselves inspired by God's authority, goodness, and perfection. *Halakhah*, a Hebrew word meaning "the way to walk," is really a prescription of

action/efforts carried out. Our walk with God is regarded as intimate, between each of us and God. What we do with the intimacy of our walk is up to us. The important thing is to "work it out with fear and trembling." (See Philippians 2:12.) The way we walk after God expresses our covenantal love for Him, which goes beyond a set of rules or laws.

I spoke in an earlier chapter of how the Lord breathed on His disciples in John 20:21 and said, "As My Father hath sent Me, even so send I you." Again, Ruach Ha Kodesh—the Breath of God—inhabits our efforts and actions. Our daily walk with God should therefore embrace the terms "Thou shalt" and "Thou shalt not." Faith apart from this walk is dead. If you ask me where my faith is today, I will answer, "It's in my walk." Whether we like it or not, we're called to perform, although the meaning of this word goes far beyond entertaining or acting. What I mean when I say that we're called upon to perform is that we're called upon to fulfill our faith or to bring it to completion through our efforts and actions. We do that through our walk with God.

Typical churchgoers are hanging on to their salvation by grace, which is good; but often they are neglecting their purpose. The minute we hear the word *purpose* we think of a great ministry or a great anointing, but I'm simply referring to humanity's purpose, that which we've been called to do during our tenure here on earth. We are called to establish and reestablish, to complete and fulfill. Let's look at how we can best do this.

THE MITZVAH (COMMANDMENT)

Deuteronomy 30:11,14 says, "For this commandment which I command thee this day, it is not hidden from thee, neither is it far off....But the word is very nigh unto thee, in thy mouth, and in thy heart, that thou mayest do it." Notice the words "that thou mayest *do it*." We all are, day by day, being transformed into a kingdom of priests and a holy nation. (See First Peter 2:9.) How is that done? We are created and formed, and then transformed. The metamorphosis comes through our walk. When we call on the name of Jesus, we're saved and given eternal life. But that doesn't transform us. Salvation is only the beginning. We must be illuminated with the message and begin to turn the wheel before the formation/transformation begins.

In the Hebrew usage, the word *mitzvah* refers to a specific divine commandment. In the Yiddish usage, it speaks of a good deed or a sense of community and corporate effort. But a *mitzvah* is much more meaningful than a rule or good deed. It is said that to perform a *mitzvah* (obey a commandment) is to reinforce the power of one's covenant with God. It purges and shapes us, and it gives us a godly mind-set and outlook on life. It is a vital part of the renewing of the mind, spoken of in Romans 12:2. Performing a *mitzvah* helps tear down the conditioning and opinions of the past. How many people have we met who seem to love God with all their heart but just can't seem to shake their past? They not only dwell on it, they continue to live in it. They can't seem to forgive and let go so they can move on. That's because they haven't understood the deeper truths of victory on earth. To think in terms of living to obey the commandments will profoundly change us, so much so that a serious Jew will get up in the morning looking for a *mitzvah* to do or perform. The system taught and applied to this thought is *halakhah* (the way to walk): "Thou shalt" and "Thou shalt not."

There are some who don't understand the reasoning behind my researching the Hebrew mind-set and interpretation. As I mentioned earlier, Jesus was a Hebrew, and He lived out these customs and systems. I understand there are people who are opposed to systems, and yet these same people will go out and purchase a new organizer every year for their calendaring and planning. I find that these Jewish systems give us a semblance of order for our walk. There is a way we should walk, and it is a pathway to holiness—*halakhah*. There is a way for that walk—the *mitzvot* (commandments). What does walking according to *halakhah* do? It establishes and reestablishes. It restores and changes us far beyond our temporary weekly feedings at church. This happens because what we are taught becomes a way of life and, eventually, creates a permanent change that causes us to perceive our past, present, and future with different eyes. It gives us "spiritual personality." It shapes and prepares us for glory. And it causes us to bear fruit that remains.

As we enter into covenant with God, we are called on to live out His *mitzvot*, or commandments. He, in turn, assumes responsibility for our presence in the world. When I perform a *mitzvah,* I am obeying and acting out a commandment. This becomes my *way* to transformation. I am saved by grace, but it is through my efforts, obedience, and works that I am changed from glory to glory. Remember, James said that faith without works is dead. He also said in James 2:19-20, "Thou believest that there is one God; thou doest well: the devils also believe, and tremble. But wilt thou know, O vain man, that faith without works is dead?" We are to be holy for He is holy. (See Leviticus 11:44.) How? We allow ourselves to be transformed by obeying God and walking as we should.

Just how realistic is it to think anyone could actually live that way? What about our human limitations? I am referring here to walking in the way—the only way. That means walking as Jesus walked, with *the way* living inside us, guiding and enabling us to walk as God has called us to walk—on the holy pathway, *halakhah.* The problem with most of us is that we have not understood the depth of the way, and therefore we miss the importance of observing *halakhah.* This is the revelation that Ruach Ha Kodesh is bringing to the Church in this hour. Why has God chosen to reveal this great truth to us now? It is because very soon He is coming back for a Bride without spot or wrinkle, and that means a Bride who walks as He has called us to walk.

THE EARTH IS THE LORD'S

To establish and restore, or reestablish, is part of humanity's purpose on earth. Once we understand this we begin to sense our own personal purpose in life. Remember, so far we have determined that there is a progressive move within the anointing that comes through the Breath of God. Everything having to do with the prophetic and the anointing is progressive. In other words, when we are moving or operating within the prophetic and the anointing, we will see *upward movement.*

I would like to shed some light on what I believe to be a missing link in possessing our inheritance. Psalm 24:1a says, "The earth is the Lord's, and the fulness thereof." This means that everything created belongs to the Lord—all in all, including *all* humanity. When we think in terms of land, we must realize this entire planet belongs to God. He created it for us, but it belongs to Him. There are basically two reasons for the land. One is to provide our sustenance (food, water, etc.), and the other is to provide a place for us to live and walk (*halakhah*)—in other words, a place where we can live for Him, fulfilling His commandments.

It was not until very recently that I began to understand my purpose. I remember hearing that humanity was created to worship God, but what did that mean to me? At the time I thought it meant singing praises to Him. Many of us, in fact, grow up in the Lord believing that worship is through music alone. Although music is a vital part of worship, true worship consists of serving God with all our heart. In the ancient *Qumran* community (a sect of Judaism, many of whom came to believe in Yeshua—Jesus—as the Messiah) they practiced "clock worship" to the Lord. In other words, they studied and discussed God's Word around the clock. Studying the Word of God is a form of worship. Praying is also a form of worship, as is participating in music and singing to God. But worship also has to do with our behavior. It has to do with obeying the commandments and fulfilling His Word.

Human beings are made up of spirit/soul, and body. When Jesus referred to worshiping God "in spirit and in truth" in John 4:23, He was referring to our entire being, meaning that a unified Body of Christ would worship God as one—with spirit/soul, and body. This is why singing together is a part of worship. If we sing, we put sound to that which is within us. If we feel a healthy emotion rise, it is part of our soul reaching out in expression. If we read and study the Word of God, we are opening all our senses to the changing power of the truth of God. If we dance before Him or lift our hands in worship, we are expressing ourselves with the flesh He created to house us. Every part of us is then worshiping the Lord. Our behavior is what responds to His commandments, and commandments obeyed, along with the fulfilled Word, is what brings true holiness. To stand for righteousness is to worship the Lord.

At the time of creation, everything was holy and beautiful. Soon after that, however, it was all tainted by man's ideas, sin, and idolatry. At the time of the fall of man, everything holy became polluted, and it continued to become progressively worse with time. Because the earth is the Lord's and He created it for us, I believe our job is to restore it to its original state, which was holy, not polluted.

How can this be done? How can one change a generation or a culture that believes in abortion and sheds innocent blood, or allows murderers and sex offenders to go free? How can one change that which has been bred and accepted into a culture? Although I'll admit we probably can't do it in one lifetime or generation, we can still make a difference.

It is a well-known fact, depending on the geographic area, that more than 50 percent of all Christians in America don't vote. Some figure they can't change anything with one vote. Others don't want to deal with the issues affecting their cities because they are too distasteful. I'm not promoting political action, but I am promoting holy action. We must be holy in all we think, do, and say—and we must promote holiness by standing for righteousness.

One year, during election time, the Lord spoke to me about not muzzling His mouth. I didn't quite understand it at the time, but I realize now what He was attempting to convey. God speaks through us—not only through our voices, but also through our actions. If there are two people running for a legislative office and one is doing everything possible to enforce God's commandments while the other is not, what do we do with our voices? Do we use them to speak out for God's righteousness, or do we muzzle them for fear of what others might think or because we think our voices won't do any good?

Let's say someone godly gets into a legislative seat for one term. How do we know if, during that term, there will come a great outpouring of grace for the community to respond to the Breath of God? By not standing for righteousness through a voting opportunity, we "muzzle the mouth of God." What we do for that moment could affect generations to come.

I know many Christians feel believers shouldn't get involved in politics, but Romans 13:1-7 tells us that government is an ordained institution of God. True, politics has so infiltrated government that the Church wants nothing to do with it; however, I believe it is also true that politics has infiltrated many of the local churches. The election process is one small avenue that gives us an opportunity to fulfill God's *mitzvot*, to be godly witnesses to an ungodly world, and to unveil Christ to those who need Him so desperately.

When I first began working in the political arena years ago, I was so gung ho that I constantly preached about the necessity of getting involved. Since then I've grown up a bit and realize that not everyone is called to run for office or to work on a campaign or in a legislative office. But some are. The Lord wants His presence in every aspect of life, including government, because the earth—including everything in it—belongs to Him.

There are four institutions ordained by God: family, Church, government, and Israel. Why would He not want His people affecting all four areas? How else can we be holy and bring holiness into a situation except to get involved in that situation? How else can we restore to their original state those things that the enemy of God has polluted?

Jesus said we are to worship the Lord in spirit and in truth. We can no longer fool ourselves into thinking that worshiping God is only related to music, or that being holy happens only within the confines of a church building. Holiness may be a by-product of being a part of God's Church, but there are some people sitting in the United States House of Representatives today who exhibit more holiness and godliness than some attending Thursday night choir practice. By walking in the way (*halakhah*), we become holy because we are walking as He has called us to walk, and He is holy. By walking in the way, we begin to do our part to restore things to their original state of holiness. We can't do it all, but when we do our part we are participating in restoring to holiness what has been His all along.

We can't effectively possess the land if we don't start the process of holiness within it. If we want the Breath of God to be loosed upon our city, community, or church, we must remember that "the earth is the Lord's, and the fulness thereof."

SUBDUING THE LAND

The word *subdue* in the Torah really means "inherit." Numbers 32:22-23 addresses the inheritance of the Promised Land:

And the land be subdued before the Lord: then afterward ye shall return, and be guiltless before the Lord, and before Israel; and this land shall be your possession before the Lord. But if ye will not do so, behold, ye have sinned against the Lord: and be sure your sin will find you out.

Let's observe the process of subduing, or inheriting, the land. Originally all the land—the earth and everything in it—belonged to God. Then God gave it to man, who, through his sin and rebellion against God, passed it on to the devil, who promptly took dominion. When Jesus came to give His life for us, the legal rights reverted to God, but now it's up to us to take it back. We must inherit/subdue it for ourselves. But how do we do that when it has already been dominated by sin and curse?

In the story of the burning bush in Exodus 3, Moses was completely perplexed by his first prophecy. In verse 2 he saw the Angel of the Lord in a burning bush. In verse 5, when Moses tried to get closer, the Lord told him to take off his shoes for he was standing on holy ground. According to Jewish literature, God told Moses to remove his shoes, because the ground was holy and God had a destiny for it. Mose's action would commit him to walking with God to take the land. Moses understood what God was saying, and he took off his shoes and committed to the destiny of the land. This was at Horeb, or Mount Sinai, where later the Torah was given to the Israelites. It was a holy place, significant, for there the Lord would descend to meet with Moses. But first Moses had to make a commitment to follow through on God's call and command.

Moses had a successor named Joshua. In Joshua 1:3 the Lord said to Joshua, "Every place that the sole of your foot shall tread upon, that have I given unto you." There is something significant about the feet of mankind touching soil. In this case, it meant official dominion. As Joshua and the people of God walked the land, it was symbolic of the land becoming theirs. It was symbolic of destiny and inheritance.

There are two steps involved in subduing or inheriting the land. The first is to *commit* to the destiny of the land; the second is to take dominion by *occupying*—claiming and taking up space. I believe the greatest error on our part is deserting a place assigned to us because of the atmosphere of sin that may be present. God called Moses to *commit* to the destiny of Sinai. True, along with the other Israelites, Moses traveled in circles for a while first, but when it was time to fulfill the destiny of the land, he followed through on his commitment. In addition, the destiny of the land went far beyond that geographic area. God's *mitzvot*, or commandments, which were birthed through the oral tradition and later committed to writing, comprised the Torah, and they would affect countless future generations.

On every possible occasion we are to fulfill God's commandments. After all, what was the reason the Lord gave those commandments to His people? God's purpose has always been to redeem man from the curse of sin and, through the guidelines of the commandments as well as our response and behavior toward them, we *restore* that which once was established.

The Breath of God was released upon His Church at Pentecost for the fulfillment of the Law and the Prophets. As we obey His commandments, we begin the restoration of the earth and *all* its fullness. As we turn the wheel, we join efforts with His heart to fulfill that which has been spoken by His prophets. We *commit* to the destiny of the land, and we *occupy* until He comes.

How do we subdue/inherit the land? We work toward restoring it to its original state by committing to its destiny and by occupying. We must inherit that which is His and was created for us because "the earth is the Lord's, and the fulness thereof." When the fulness of God comes into our city or church, this is part of our expected response and behavior.

The Breath of God, Ruach Ha Kodesh, is breathing on His Bride to establish and restore (reestablish). The ownership issue must be reestablished through the act of holiness as we walk in the way (*halakhah*) and obey (perform) His commandments (*mitzvot*). The predominantly Gentile Church may not like adopting Hebrew ways, but this is the way our Lord was reared and taught, and it's the way He lived and walked. Therefore, when we walk the same way, it becomes a "walk of obedience." Our inheritance depends on it. Holiness will reestablish the earth and everything in it because it belongs to the Lord, and He created it for us. The destiny of the earth, our lives, and future generations is not dependent on the devil and the world. It is dependent on His Body here on earth. This is why the Breath of God has been grieved for years. The fullness of the Godhead has been driven away because of the improper response and behavior of His people. He has been rejected, and His Spirit has been abused.

We have lost touch with our Covenant as we walk through a life that compromises even the smallest commandments. Jesus came to fulfill the Law and the Prophets—not to bring bondage, but to bring freedom. It is said by many Hebrew scholars and rabbis that to get on the pathway (*halakhah*) is to *already* be holy. Is it because, in and of ourselves, we are? No, it is because we have made a commitment to destiny, to God's will for our lives. We are on the way, and He is the way. We are called on to restore what is His. This includes souls. All humanity is His creation. Not one soul should burn in hell. Not one soul should remain backslidden. Can one generation accomplish all that? No, but that's no reason not to try. Everything we do should be directed toward helping the generation we live in, which will in turn affect generations to come.

As we address the establishing and reestablishing of the framework of God's Kingdom, we must understand what it means to work. Our work is to establish and restore. God breathed on us to send us to work on the way home, to bring things back to their original state. The earth is His, all humanity is His, and all creation belongs to Him. It has been neglected, tampered with, torn down, and forgotten. Our churches and ministries have a purpose. Our breath has a purpose, and that purpose is to establish and reestablish (restore), not so we can build our own kingdoms, but His.

Because the Church has not understood its "work" assignment, there has been great "division in vision." Our motives must be focused, for without this work, our faith is dead. In Ecclesiastes 1 King Solomon spoke of "vanity of vanities," and asked in verse 3, "What profit hath a man of all his labour which he taketh under the sun?" Solomon, of course, was speaking of worldly labor. In verse 14 he continued, "I have seen all the works that are done under the sun; and, behold, all is vanity and vexation of spirit." There is no real profit under the sun in worldly labor. But, sad to say, there is just as much worldly labor going on in the Church as there is in the world. Most of that labor is not done to restore, but to build—not the Kingdom of God, but our own kingdoms! Until that changes, there will be no "fruit that remains" produced from our labors.

I believe the Spirit of the Lord has been grieved by the worldly labors in the Church. How He longs for the "fruit that remains"! How He desires to see us get what He created for us. The ignorance of the Church has made her easy prey for the enemy. The work of the world is vanity, and it profits nothing. The work of the Spirit will always restore and build, producing fruit that remains. "For God shall bring every work into judgment, with every secret thing, whether it be good, or whether it be evil" (Eccles. 12:14). The Lord spoke a word to me concerning this very thing:

> *"Do you not know, Beloved, that every knee shall fold and every tongue will confess that I am Lord of lords? Many will run from the truth, and in their race shall find the truth. Many will testify beforehand of the truth, run from it in compromise, trampling that which is Holy underfoot. Many will renounce truth at its sound for the hardness of their heart. But **all** will fold their knee to me and confess that I am **Elohim**, Creator and Sustainer of all, encompassing all. 'Be ye Holy; for I am Holy.' I have made a **way** for you. Look beyond that which man has presented to you, and worship Me in spirit and in truth."*

Everything within the Breath of God is progressive. It is a process, a metamorphosis, not only for the Church but also for the earth. It begins with illumination, a "catching on fire." And it should be followed by a turning of the wheel, a setting in motion, regardless of the "squeaks." Finally, God wants His work established and His Kingdom built. The Lord is calling on His Church to take it *all the way*, to commit to the destiny of the land as Moses did. This is why He desires to impart the fullness of the Godhead upon this spiritual generation chosen as a holy nation.

One church is illuminated and never moves on, while another moves to the wheel and stops when it squeaks from allowing man to dictate the vision God gave them; few move on to establish and reestablish (restore and rebuild). But God is faithful; a remnant will go all the way to become that "perfect match" for the Breath of God's fullness in this hour.

The Breath of God is progressive. If we are not experiencing His Presence in fullness, chances are we may have grieved Him, and we must repent so we can move on in His holiness—walking in *halakhah*—establishing, restoring, and rebuilding, as we commit to God's destiny for His creation.

Chapter 4

HEROES FROM THE HISTORY OF FAITH:
Riding the Wave

It wasn't until recently that I was able to put into words my interest in the "heroes of the faith." The Church has received many words about the "wave" of God's Spirit. Every pastor and minister wants to be in the wave. People in the local church are hungering to experience the wave. It's one thing to jump into a wave in the ocean, but there's an all-time high in actually learning how to ride that wave. If we catch a wave just right, it will take us all the way onto shore.

In the parable of the net in Matthew 13:47-50, Jesus talked about filling the net with fish and drawing it to shore. One of the object lessons in this parable is that as many souls as possible should be drawn to shore. If we can catch a wave of His Spirit and ride it in to shore, how much better will the catch or harvest be? Learning about biblical and modern-day heroes is a giant step in learning to ride the wave.

ANCESTRAL FAITH

The Holy Spirit and the Word of God teach us about those of the "household of faith." By understanding what these giants of the faith did right, as well as what they did wrong, we learn how to effectively ride the wave to shore. Jumping in the water isn't enough; we've got to learn to ride the wave all the way.

How did these heroes of faith think and operate? What were they like? What made them different? The purpose of this chapter is not to address or examine the individual lives of these heroes, as many books have already been written on that topic, but it is to address the corporate traits in their lives and ministries that helped them ride the wave of His Spirit.

First, let's examine the Hebrew word *pela*. This word really speaks of ancestral faith. The study of ancestral faith reveals trends that affect the people of God. Although God never changes, and though the way we approach Him never changes (through faith), God has moved in different ways throughout the years, and there seem to be times in history when faith for miracles or for provision and/or abundance was stronger or more evident than at others.

During the 1980s, faith for deliverance was at an all-time high. People were being set free, books were written on the topic, and teachings were revised to focus on this subject. Eventually, however, the Church seemed to move from a focus on deliverance to a focus on spiritual warfare. Again, books were written on the topic, and teachings were revised. These are examples of trends instigated by the Spirit of God to stir the Body of Christ. As the people of God search and study the topic of the hour, they are illuminated in a particular area, and faith begins to grow.

I can remember when I started to operate in the area of deliverance. Prior to that time, ministering in that area was the farthest thing from my mind. But while working for Pat Robertson I received a telephone call from a Southern California pastor who wanted to meet with me. He told me he had a powerful spiritual warfare prayer meeting happening weekly, and he felt led by God to meet with me regarding some items I was working on. When I arrived at his office we began to share about some of the things God was doing in our lives and ministries. In the process of our discussion he talked with me about the subject of deliverance. One thing led to another, and he allowed me to hear some audiotapes of some of the deliverance sessions.

I remember being very interested as I listened to the tapes, but I felt a bit apprehensive at the thought of such an encounter myself. Yet something stirred within me, something I would describe as a "healthy hunger," instigated by God. As I talked to the Lord about it, searched Scripture, and studied books on the topic, my faith for this type of encounter increased, as did the reality of my authority and protection in Christ. God was preparing me for what was ahead. Even today, the faith for this area of ministry remains stronger than ever in me, and it is very much operable. People might have called it a "trend" for me, but God designated this trend for a purpose.

This type of process has repeated itself throughout the years within the Body of Christ. But I believe the day has now come when the people of God are stirring with a "fullness faith." It is a time for fullness, and God is bestowing the gift of faith for this hour. The Body of Christ is no longer stirring just for healing, deliverance, or prosperity. This is a *pela* type of faith, an ancestral faith that confronts the impossible. *Pela* speaks of incidents such as Abraham putting his only son, Isaac, on the altar in response to God's directive. But *pela* doesn't come only through trials and hardships. I believe *pela* can rise up in something as simple as God calling us to step out and do something we never thought we could.

My brother Danny Diaz is now the pastor of Victorious Living Christian Center, a growing church in California. But once he was an alcoholic with a violent personality. My sister-in-law Yolanda, Danny's wife, prayed and believed God to deliver him from that lifestyle. At the time it looked impossible, but the God of the impossible delivered Danny and birthed him into the Kingdom. Yolanda was ecstatic! Still, she never imagined either of them would be involved in ministry. Today, not only is Danny a pastor, Yolanda is the leader of the women's ministry group in their church. Those who knew them before recognize the change in their lives as the mark of the miraculous. And it came about through a *pela* type of faith.

When I gave birth to my son Albert, the doctor told me he was dead and said I might not make it as well. I lay there on that hospital table, bleeding to death, and prayed to my God. Medically, the situation looked impossible. I was only a child myself, with my intellect and knowledge shaken, but I had an overwhelming love for God inside me that would not be shaken. Regardless of what the doctor said, I never thought for one moment that God would allow my son or me to die. I was determined we would live, even though it was an "impossible possibility." Today my son stands 6'3", loves Jesus, and has a powerful prophetic anointing developing on his life, while I am prophesying God's Word all over the world. God is faithful, but at the time I was lying on that hospital bed, things looked impossible.

I believe *pela* is tailored to our individuality. I believe this for two reasons. First, God knows everything about us; and second, faith is synonymous with trust. I once read an analogy that said, "To believe I exist is not necessarily to believe I am trustworthy." In other words, my existence does not make me a person who can be trusted. We all have neighbors where we live, and we know they exist. We may see them when they leave for work in the morning or when they do their gardening on Saturday. But the question is, do we trust them? Would we trust them with our finances, our possessions, the intimate details of our existence, even our families and our own lives? *Faith is not just believing, but trusting.*

There are a lot of people, saved and unsaved, who believe God exists, but they don't trust Him. Most of the people in the Church today believe God exists, but they don't really trust Him. This is why we don't see more of the miraculous. True, it takes a certain amount or type of faith to believe someone we've never seen before exists, but *pela* is more than that. It is an all-out, no-matter-the-circumstances trust. It is the type of faith that produces biblical heroes.

Hebrews 11:6 says, "Without faith it is impossible to please Him: for he that cometh to God must believe that He is, and that He is a rewarder of them that diligently seek Him." First we must believe *He is*, and then we must believe *He will*. In order to live life on earth victoriously, we must trust and believe that God will do what He has promised to do. And our faithful Father will see that we are presented with the right opportunities to learn that great lesson of *pela*.

History demonstrates the truth about faith. In every age the Church's response to faith appears to have been conditioned by cultural circumstances. The possibility of a reinterpretation of faith during any generation is unheard of because of our conditioning; in fact, it seems impossible. This is what we call the "presentation of the impossible possibility." We're a conditioned people, and when the Breath of God comes in with a deeper illumination of something we've previously been taught, we become stubborn in our ways. We critique what we don't understand because it's foreign and distant to our conditioning.

Please understand, I'm not speaking of receiving "new revelation"; I'm referring to *deeper revelation*. The Breath of God brings deeper illumination/revelation to our lives, and deeper revelation always stretches us and shakes our intellect. God intends to stretch and shake us in order to prepare us for what's ahead. Our intellect has been our problem for too long. The conditioning of our culture within the Church has created roadblocks to receiving the things of God. Throughout history *pela* has introduced deeper truths from God, as well as possible reinterpretations of what has already been taught. Denominational theology is not, nor will it ever be, open to *pela*. The majority of the Pharisees and other religious leaders weren't open to it in Jesus' day; sadly, that hasn't changed much. Within our denominations we must be willing to step into what God is doing at the moment, regardless of whether or not it lines up with man's past teaching, culture, or corporate interpretation.

In retrospect, we need to view these two areas closely to understand the times in which we live. First, this is the time of fullness—in *every* area. Although we could argue that it's always been God's time for His people to respond to and receive His Breath, the people of God have previously been limited in the amount of revelation they received from God. But as I write this book, I believe there is a "fullness revelation" being released upon the readers by the Breath of God. This revelation brings a desire to set that fullness in motion and to restore and establish the Kingdom of God. We are no longer just experiencing trends of faith for abundance or healing. This is the time for the faith of impossible possibilities. This is *pela*—ancestral faith restored.

The second point is this: With this desire for fullness comes a disclosure of reality that illuminates and brings deeper faith. This illumination will shake our culture, our mind-set, and most of our man-made church doctrines.

In Chapter 3 I spoke of restoring and establishing the fullness of creation as our God-given inheritance. I speak now of the restoration of ancestral faith. Anytime a specific anointing is released, revelation must first touch our hearts. We have been filled with man's ideas of what faith is and how it pleases God. (See Hebrews 11:6.) As a result of man's teaching, anything that shakes our prior thinking is viewed as error. We close our hearts to the deeper truths that bring us into the fullness of God's revelation for this hour. The Word of God doesn't change; neither does the revelation of that Word. But the depth of revelation and understanding of the Word *does* change. Therefore, we must be willing to go deeper into the truths of God.

Faith in biblical days was different than the faith we have today. Smith Wigglesworth once said, "The problem with our faith is that we have too many remedies." God has been good to us; we're a blessed people. But remedies sometimes take our eyes off the reality of trusting God. Ancestral faith—*pela*—caused people to trust God.

Now it's true that God is merciful, and for this I'm grateful. But He has been grieved with a Church that *believes* He exists but doesn't *trust* Him. Will He have to teach us to trust through difficult circumstances? In His mercy, Ruach Ha Kodesh is being released to illuminate a spoiled Bride, a Jewish princess who has been handed everything on a silver platter, ever receiving but seldom grateful. I'm referring, of course, to the Christian Church, particularly in America. Remedies are not the answer; God is the answer. Our focus for too long has been on the remedy and not the Source. Not only do we ask amiss (see Jas. 4:3), we think amiss. Sound doctrine has been tampered with for the sake of the "stroking of the flesh." *Pela* is foreign to today's pampered believer, but these are the days of the restoration of ancestral faith.

Throughout the Bible we see a powerful thread of influence in individuals called upon to believe the impossible possibility. Many believe that God Himself presented impossible possibilities to His people in order to bring them to a place of truly trusting Him. The best place to read briefly about some of these individuals is in Hebrews 11 (sometimes referred to as "The Hall of Fame for the Heroes of Faith"). Each one of these individuals was presented with *pela* at one time or another. They all were challenged with that which shook their intellect and knowledge, yet their response affected generations to come. Their cutting-edge task/mission was beyond the norm, stretching people, places, and situations. *Pela* demanded great feats and great faith. *Pela* broke all barriers of tradition, producing many miracles, signs, and wonders. *Pela* presented itself in the face of adversity. It presented itself to confound what the person and community thought they already knew. The person stepping out in this type of faith was, without a doubt, "on the edge."

When *pela* presents itself, so must the enabling grace of God; and when enabling grace presents itself, the breath of Ruach Ha Kodesh has been released. These heroes of the faith were on the edge, affecting future generations, including ours today. These heroes were operating under the direction of the heart of God. They were oblivious to danger, persecution, and exposure. *Pela* can operate only in a person or church willing to go deeper into God.

Ancestral faith always dealt with individuals and families, not with peoples and tribes. Out of a faceless generation, history brings forth Abraham, Isaac, and Jacob. This is the story of a family that had received the Breath of God. Abraham—still called Abram at that point—was first presented with *pela* while his ancestors worshiped false gods. (See Joshua 24:2.) Their pagan religion seemed to have prevailed over all existence. But Genesis 12:1 records that Abram was called by God to leave all past associations behind and go forth into a new country, away from everyone in his culture. He was to be set apart—sanctified—for God's special purpose. This was *pela* presenting itself. God promised Abram he would have divine favor and great posterity, but he had to trust God in order for that to happen. And so Abram stepped out on the edge. Abram (meaning "exalted father") was called on to respond to the sent Breath of God, and he did. As a result, his name was changed to Abraham ("father of many nations" or "father of multitudes"), and he became the father of a new spiritual race.

Isaac, a product of *pela*, was born to Abraham and Sarah as a result of God's promise and covenant. (See Genesis 15:4-6.) Isaac became a sort of "fruit of faith." He was the promised seed that brought forth Jacob, who was later transformed into Israel. This family was endowed with the threefold (three degrees of the spirit of prophecy) fresh Breath of God, as we see in Isaiah 43:1: "But now thus saith the Lord that created thee, O Jacob, and He that formed thee, O Israel, Fear not: for I have redeemed thee, I have called thee by thy name; thou art Mine." This family illustrated the unfolding of the three degrees of the spirit of prophecy within the Breath of God.

And then there was Moses' mother, who hid him for three months after his birth in spite of the king's command. Then she released her son to float around in a basket on the Nile, *trusting God* to protect him. (See Exodus 2-14.) This woman had been presented with *pela*. She knew the God of Israel existed, but that wasn't enough. She had to *know* that He would respond to her faith.

And so He did. Moses was raised in the courts of the Egyptians, sovereignly protected from the king's murderous command. But when Moses grew up and the time came to reveal his true identity, he chose to forsake Egypt, even though he knew he might have to face the wrath of the people. God had called him as an instrument of deliverance for the people of Israel, and he took the first step of *pela*. When God later appeared to him in the burning bush, Moses took off his shoes to walk on holy ground and got hold of the power in the sprinkled blood of the Lamb, which would protect the firstborn of God's people. Moses stepped out on the edge, though it made no sense to those who knew him. Even Moses had his doubts, telling God he could not adequately express himself. He was facing an impossible possibility, but he stepped out in *pela*, and God was faithful to see him through.

And then there was Joshua, Moses' successor. This man Joshua had the audacity to ask his followers to walk silently around Jericho for seven days, and then shout. (See Joshua 6.) God told Joshua the great walls of the city would come down, so Joshua stepped out on the edge. What if the walls hadn't fallen? Can you imagine a pastor asking the congregation to go into the city and march around for days at a time, saying nothing, only hanging on to God's promise that at the end of the silent march, if everyone would shout, every sexually oriented or occult business would immediately tumble to the ground? It would take great faith for the pastor and the congregation. And yet that's exactly the situation Joshua faced. Many thoughts, even doubts, must have crossed his mind, but still he continued to move forward and trust God. That trust went far beyond just believing that God existed; Joshua had to trust Him completely.

Elijah, known as the "prophet of fire," got in King Ahab's pitiful face and prophesied that a drought and famine would come upon the land. (See First Kings 17:1-7.) As we discussed earlier, Elijah housed within himself the abundance of rain that would eventually break the drought. *Pela* gave the prophet the courage to speak forth God's message. *Pela* caused him to challenge the false prophets of his day. (See

First Kings 18:20-40.) Elijah stood up in the face of adversity and told them all in verse 24, "The God that answereth by fire, let him be God."

Can you imagine calling the White House today and requesting a personal meeting with the president, explaining that you have a word from the Lord for the nation, then meeting with him and speaking judgment on the land? It is very possible you would have Secret Service agents putting a brand-new tight coat on you and escorting you off to a place of intense scrutiny. But Elijah housed a message from God, and he did not water it down, but rather prophesied it like a trumpet blast.

Elisha, Elijah's successor, clung tightly to Elijah in order to receive his impartation, or gifting/anointing, from God. There were many other young prophets watching and receiving instruction from Elijah, but it was Elisha who determined to do more than watch and listen to the great prophet. Elisha followed Elijah closely, refusing to leave his side and trusting God to pass Elijah's anointing to him, regardless of what anyone else said or thought about his behavior. His *pela* was rewarded when he received from God the mantle of Elijah's anointing.

Hannah was barren and depressed. (See First Samuel 1:1–2:11.) She went to the house of God and received faith to conceive and bear a child, a hero of faith who would alter the course of history. Through this child Samuel, future government and politics were changed and the anointing of the spirit of prophecy came forth. Hannah was presented with *pela*, a stirring within her heart that led her to the house of God to pray. There she confronted the impossible possibility of her life, and God used this woman to bring a new wave of His Spirit into history.

David, as Saul's successor to the throne of Israel, understood his covenant and overthrew the Philistine's giant Goliath. (See First Samuel 17.) The question David asked in verse 26, when confronted by this giant, was, "Who is this uncircumcised Philistine?" David was presented with *pela*; in response, David not only *believed* in but also *trusted* his God. He understood the power of covenant and the faithfulness of the Covenant Maker. Operating in *pela*, David defeated the giant and moved toward fulfilling the destiny for which he had been called and anointed by God.

And what about Shadrach, Meshach, and Abednego, who would not worship the golden image erected by Nebuchadnezzar? (See Daniel 3.) These men, faced with being thrown into the fiery furnace if they refused to worship the idol, chose instead to trust God, even if it meant losing their lives.

Daniel was thrown into the lion's den for disobeying the king's decree and praying to his God. (See Daniel 6.) He knew the probable consequences of his disobedience, yet he trusted God, and God delivered him.

All these heroes of the faith—even those who paid with their lives—knew that, apart from faith, it is impossible to please God. It was *pela*, ancestral faith, a faith of fullness—not a trend of faith for healing, prosperity, deliverance, or open doors—that would carry them through. They not only believed God existed, but also that He would be faithful, regardless of the circumstances. This type of faith was the result of having received the Breath of God. And this type of faith goes hand in hand with the anointing of fullness.

The Church thus far has looked at faith only for the purpose of receiving, but the days are here when it is time to look at faith for the purpose of giving. We have been a stingy, self-absorbed people, viewing only a partial picture of the covenant/partnership between God and man. We are so narrow minded when it comes to our covenant that we have limited God and what He can do with us as we endeavor to build His Kingdom. The more we stretch, the more He responds. We can't please Him without the stretch! This is not about believing God for more money or possessions; this is about receiving the fullness of God for the fullness of times! And for these times there is a fullness anointing.

When *pela* presents itself, it is always accompanied by enabling grace, which is the Breath of God. In order to do the greater works Jesus said we would do, in order to see creative miracles, the healing of the sick, and the raising of the dead, we need the Breath of God in our lives. This is Ruach Ha Kodesh, the Sacred Breath that brings a progressive anointing of fullness, an anointing of enabling grace, an endowment of power from on High.

The biblical heroes of faith were endued with power from God. They had an anointing of enabling grace. These ancestral heroes were operating under the power of Ruach Ha Kodesh. The fullness available in that day was upon them, but there was more to come because everything in the Word of God is progressive. Our anointing is progressive, our holiness is progressive, our walk is progressive. We're on the *way*, and we have the Spirit of God within us to take us home. And it began when we were illuminated with a truth from God.

There are those who are illuminated with a truth about holiness but have no truth about prosperity. Others are illuminated with a truth about healing but don't understand deliverance. As I said, everything is progressive. Once we're illuminated in one area, if we begin to apply the progressive action within the Breath of God (illumination, turning the wheel, and establishing), we eventually discover truths in other areas. It's an all-progressive process because we're on our *way*. He who is within us is taking us home.

As time goes by, there is a measurable increase of illumination and anointing upon the Church. This is why the Lord spoke of us doing greater works. (See John 14:12.) It's not that we can be more powerful than Jesus was when He walked the earth, but rather that the era in His day here on earth didn't require the same measure of illumination and anointing. He portrayed the actions of the apostles as examples of what was available during that time. But as we live in this present era, there is a need for greater works, an increase in power, and an evident anointing. The fullness of God's anointing depends on one thing: God's prophetic clock. The biblical heroes of the faith were models of the time and the fullness of God for that space in history.

Today we're living in a different space in history. We continue to work toward the same things, but it's a different time with a different measure of fullness. The adversary has launched a strategic, wicked plan that has targeted family, Church, government, and Israel. There must be a deeper understanding of the times and strategy for battle. Everything is progressively working together to fit within the parameters of His design and purpose; the collective Body of Christ is the vehicle God will use to complete that progressive work. And we, as individuals, are the vehicles He will use for the restoration and establishing of ancestral faith.

Spiritual Heritage

Through His prophet, the Lord said in Isaiah 51:1b, "Look unto the rock whence ye are hewn [carved]." God was reminding His people to take time to trace their spiritual heritage. Again in Romans 11:18b, the apostle Paul reminded the believers in Rome that they weren't the ones who supported the root, but the root supported them. I believe if we would allow the root to support our existence, if we would take the time to trace our spiritual heritage, we wouldn't be so inconsistent in our faith walk. We can learn so much by observing others' walk with God.

I remember feeling angry when, as a new Christian, I heard individuals rejoice over a victory one Sunday, then complain and murmur over an unpaid bill the next. One of the questions I heard most often was, "I tithe, so why am I in this condition?" When I hear people affirming themselves and questioning God's principles, I know they're unstable, insecure, and bound by fear. Momentary victory determines their daily joy and peace. If everything is going well, they rejoice and praise God. If the going gets tough, they complain and murmur. They praise God only when things are going according to their own plan. These individuals know nothing about their spiritual heritage.

Most of us in the Church rarely take time to really understand our spiritual heritage. Abraham was referred to by the Hebrew word *avinu,* meaning "our father." Paul stated in Galatians 3:29 that we belong to Christ; therefore, we are Abraham's seed and heirs to the promises of God's covenant with Abraham. I belong to Christ, which makes me a daughter of Abraham. That is my spiritual heritage. But what does that mean?

In Second Timothy 1:5 Paul wrote to Timothy, his spiritual son, and said, "I call to remembrance the unfeigned faith that is in thee, which dwelt first in thy grandmother Lois, and thy mother Eunice." Paul was referring to spiritual heritage, a lineage of "unfeigned" (pure) faith, *pela,* ancestral faith passed down from one generation to the next. In verse 3 of that same chapter Paul said, "I thank God, whom I serve from my forefathers with pure conscience." Paul was speaking of serving, as did his forefathers, in purity of faith. He was speaking of his spiritual heritage, and he was thanking God that Timothy was keeping up the faith of his ancestors.

Throughout the Word of God there is an unfolding of ancestral faith. Although that faith is supposed to grow stronger, it has instead grown weaker. The further the Church moved from its spiritual heritage, the further we moved from operating in ancestral faith.

Galatians 3:1-2 challenges us with the following questions: "O foolish Galatians, who hath bewitched you, that ye should not obey the truth...? ...Received ye the Spirit [fullness] by the works of the law, or by the hearing of faith [ancestral faith]?" The purpose is plain; they had departed from ancestral faith and were bewitched demonically (influenced) by man's doctrine. The apostle reminded them in verses 6-7 that, just as Abraham believed God and it was accounted to him for righteousness, so it is for all people of faith, for those are the children of Abraham.

Verse 21 of that same chapter asks, "Is the law then against the promises of God?" The answer comes quickly: "God forbid!" Verse 26 then tells us who we are *by faith*: "For ye are all the children of God by faith in Christ Jesus." Then, in verse 29, we read again of spiritual heritage: "And if ye be Christ's, then are ye Abraham's seed, and heirs according to the promise."

What does it mean to be an heir? The Hebrew word that represents heir is *yarash*, which, simply put, means to possess. If we are Christ's, then we are Abraham's seed, and "possessors" according to the promise. God promised He would make Abraham a great nation. He told him *all* families in this nation on earth would be blessed. He told Abraham he would give to him and to *all his seed* the land of Canaan. (See Genesis 12:1-3,7.)

The land of Canaan is referred to as a "sanctuary" in Exodus 15:17 and a "land of promise" in Hebrews 11:9. It is a place of great sustenance and provision, and it is promised to *all* of Abraham's seed. This is a spiritual heritage that began with our father Abraham. The promises traveled through history with intensity as the world prepared for the Messiah. Promises evolved out of promises, and the world waited for the promise of restoration—the new and better covenant. A Savior had been promised. Luke 1:32-33 states, "He shall be great, and shall be called the Son of the Highest: and the Lord God shall give unto Him the throne of His father David [spiritual heritage]: and He shall reign over the house of Jacob for ever; and of His kingdom there shall be no end."

With the Messiah would come a promise. There had been glimpses of this promise in the pages of biblical history, but this was different. This would be the fulfillment of what Jesus spoke of in Luke 24:49: "And, behold, I send the promise of My Father upon you: but tarry ye in the city of Jerusalem, until ye be endued with power from on high." Notice the wording: *I send the promise of My Father.* What could that promise be? How would it come? It would come as a blast of power and fullness, Ruach Ha Kodesh, the promise of the Father, our spiritual heritage from God, the restoration of ancestral faith. (See Acts 2.)

Oh, foolish Church that we are! Who has bewitched us? Didn't we begin in the Spirit? Do we now think we can be completed in the flesh? To fall away from the faith is more than backsliding in some outward, obvious way; it is also a departure from *trusting God.* We have become a deceived Church, believing God exists, but not believing He will be faithful to His Word and His promises. We have been bewitched by easy remedies and solutions, when the only true remedy or solution is prayer. Our survival is in Him. The promised Messiah came and, after His death, resurrection, and ascension, sent to us the promise of the Father. That promise is none other than the Breath of God! Because it is from the Father, it encompasses all the fullness of the Godhead, and it is necessary to do the work of the Father, as God so clearly spoke to me:

> *"For the day is here that My Son would be glorified, and mockers would fall to their knees. The day is here that My Church would arise with feats that would cause the enemy to tremble, and the world to repent or die. I will be mocked no longer. I have chosen a people, a Holy Nation. This is My day. This is My time. World leaders will sense the reality of the times and be called to accountability. Church leaders have already sensed the reality of the times and are called to accountability. This is My day. Computers will not help you. Money will not change the seconds on My clock, and My Church will have to respond or walk away from Me. This is the fullness of the promise of the Father, coming upon His children. Remember the word spoken through My prophet Joel. There is a remnant prepared. This is My day. I will not*

tolerate the mocking any longer; I will no longer look upon compromise as I did in the past. Pray, My beloved. Pray for those lost and blinded. Pray for My leaders who continue to break bread with the world and defile My beloved Bride. Pray for those who are lukewarm, that they might be shaken within before the shaking comes from without. Pray for those souls held captive. For this army of mine will be sent, as Abraham was sent to deliver his kinsman Lot, when Lot was taken captive by the enemy. My people will take the souls and the spoil and give them back to Me. This is My day. I will bless My army and will have no use for cowards. The promise is for you and for those afar off who belong to Me. This is your spiritual heritage."

We must remember the rock from which we were carved. If we realize our spiritual heritage, we will no longer walk around with a "here today, gone tomorrow" faith. The promises made to our forefathers are for us. The promise of the Father is for all who will call on His name. This is a heritage to possess. The heroes of the faith operated with a *pela* that God desires to restore to His Church.

I believe there are many heroes of the faith who are not documented on earth, but rather in Heaven. Throughout the years there have been those who dared to step out on the edge. Today is the day for us to step into our spiritual heritage. Remember, without faith (trust) it is impossible to please God. We already believe *He is.* Now we must believe *He will.* We all have impossible possibilities, but "with God all things are possible" (Mt. 19:26), and so it is that we are called to live a life of trusting Him.

LEARN TO RIDE THE WAVE

In studying the waves of God at different intervals in American history, I've found the power of healing always encourages revival. If people know a wave of healing is possible, they come to the waters. Just as Ezekiel 47 speaks of the waters flowing from the Temple, the waters are flowing from the Throne of God. This is Living Water that brings cleansing through repentance. There is healing in this water because it is a "cleansing stream." Anytime there is pure cleansing, there is always healing. And healing always attracts the multitudes.

Most feel that it was in the 1960s that the last portion of the awesome healing revival wave of the twentieth century was loosed. After that the Breath of God came and released a new wave for biblical education. Our dear brother Oral Roberts decided he would catch that new wave, and suddenly he was moved into the educational arena. It was as though God began releasing His Breath on places that were teaching His Word, and Brother Roberts recognized it. He was presented with *pela*, and his whole ministry went into transition, as he trusted God to carry him through.

In 1971 Lester Sumrall opened a School of Evangelism that focused on deliverance. He believed there was going to be a great need for this gift to be taught for the future, and so he operated in *pela* and stepped out into the arena of trusting God. Brother Sumrall was right-on, because a few years later deliverance became a major issue.

These two men of God were "catching the wave." They were doing something that few had done before because the previous focus had been on the healing revival. The freshness of what God was doing had come with a change, as it always does.

In 1986 Pat Robertson decided to run for President of the United States. His ministry wasn't suffering and he didn't need to make a change, but God was doing something. The Church was not only asleep; it was hypnotized by the process of gradualism. I've had the pleasure of working with Pat, and I know he is a man of integrity. He often told me the decision to run for president was not easy for him, but he responded to the Breath of God as he was presented with *pela*. Pat knew he would suffer criticism, and what God had called him to do seemed an impossible possibility. But Pat's job wasn't to take the office of president; it was to awaken a sleeping Church. To do so, Pat had to step out in *pela* and trust God.

I could go on and on with examples of some of the modern-day heroes of the faith who have been presented with a form of *pela* as the whole world watched their progress. Many were called to change locations at the height of their ministry success. Others took their programs off the air because God told them to do so. They heard from God, and they responded. What they were called to do shook their intellect and astounded those around them, but they stepped out anyway. If they hadn't, they wouldn't necessarily have lost their place in the wave, but they wouldn't have *ridden* the wave. There's a difference, and to understand that difference we must learn to move with God, not with what man thinks we should do.

We've all heard the worldly axiom, "If it ain't broke, don't fix it." Terrible grammar—and not the best advice, either, at least not in God's Kingdom. As believers, we don't need to wait until something stops working before moving on to something else. When God calls us to move, we need to respond immediately, whether what we've been doing is still working or not. In other words, *we don't need to taste defeat in order to submit to change.* To be called to change when we're doing well is a sure presentation of *pela*, the impossible possibility.

If there's one thing I've noticed about all the biblical and modern-day heroes of the faith, it's that they responded to His Breath and went where they were sent. When we change with *His* flow, we "catch the wave." There are many local churches that don't understand this concept, and there are many people who won't submit to change. But in the Spirit of God, all things are possible if we just trust Him.

Whether or not God is speaking to us about change at this particular moment isn't the issue; the issue is the willingness of our heart to trust God, to walk in the faith of our forefathers. This is ancestral faith. The reason God desires to restore this type of faith to the Church is because it's time to stop building our own kingdoms and concentrate on building His. We can't do that if we won't respond to Ruach Ha Kodesh and learn to ride the wave.

We need to remember those past heroes of faith. Abraham, Moses, Elijah, David—they all had plans of their own. But God had bigger plans for them. In order to step into those plans, they had to be willing to change, even when it didn't make sense. God wants to present us with *pela*. He wants us to learn to ride the wave.

LORD, INCREASE OUR FAITH

In Luke 17:5 the disciples said to Jesus, "Increase our faith." I can remember people telling me, "Irma, whatever you do, don't ask for patience or faith." I know now that wasn't good advice because it causes fear. It holds us back from stepping out in what God has for us. It keeps us from learning to ride the wave.

First of all, gifts and virtues do not come to us by reason, but by grace. Remember, grace enables us. Grace is superior to all reason. And grace is found in the Breath of God. But negative people have painted a negative picture: If we ask for patience, we will be tried over and over again; if we ask for faith, we will find ourselves in difficult circumstances. How absurd! Do we think God is so small that He has to resign Himself to reason in order to impart a virtue or a gift? There are times God may use reason to get through to us, simply because we are so hardheaded and won't listen to His voice. And, of course, God is sovereign and can use any means He pleases to reach us. However, faith is leaving behind all reason and stepping out in obedience to God's voice. We cannot—we *must* not—walk in fear of how we are going to get what He wants us to have. We must trust Him; we must know that *He is* and that *He will*. (See Hebrews 11:6.)

I believe we need to ask God to increase our faith with mercy and grace. We have an eternal job to do in a temporal place, and for that we need faith, not reason. Faith is a conviction of the invisible, not the visible. Therefore, reason should not control us. If we're living our lives based on reason, we'll always be candidates for fear. The Breath of God releases the grace that enables us to receive all things from God. Our prayer should be, "Lord, increase our faith!"

My Hero (My Overwhelming Love)

The Word became flesh and lived among us. (See John 1:14.) In John 14:6 Jesus declared Himself to be the Way, the Truth, and the Life. He grew strong in spirit as a child, and He showed Himself to everyone as the Son of God. He shook man's intellect to the very core. His inauguration into public ministry at His baptism showed Ruach Ha Kodesh coming upon Him in the form of a dove. The heavens were opened and a voice came forth declaring the testimony and message, "This is My beloved Son, in whom I am well pleased" (Mt 3:17). He turned water into wine. (See John 2:1-11.) He became indignant in the Temple over the religious leaders' disrespect of God's house—not a popular reaction, as the buying and selling that went on in the Temple had become quite commonplace, a "cultural" thing that few questioned. (See Mark 11:15-18.) He spoke to a Samaritan woman, which in itself was almost unheard of. Not only was she a woman, she was a Samaritan, a rejected woman of a race unaccepted by the Jews. But Jesus reached out to her and told her about Living Water. He stepped out on the edge, and as a result, revival came to that town. (See John 4:1-30.)

Jesus is the perfect example of the impossible possibility, the perfect example of trusting. He is the fullness of the Godhead, the Breath of God, and the anointing of God's fullness. To *know* Him is to have life. To *trust* Him is to please God. The message of the hour is clear: Step out on the edge, and He will be with you. Trust Him, and do not lean on reason. (See Proverbs 3:5.) Just as He breathed on His disciples and sent them out, He is breathing on His Church and sending us.

Jesus began His public ministry after His baptism, and as the miracles and signs flowed, the philosophers and religious leaders were shaken. He loved much, was filled with compassion, and wasn't afraid to touch the "undesirables." He raised the dead, expelled demons, and confounded what He termed in Matthew 12:34 and 23:33 a "generation of vipers." He spoke to the wind, He walked on water, and He allowed the fools of His day to take Him and slaughter Him as a Lamb—the very Lamb of God. He took His blood and purchased us and set us free. Our Master, our Beloved, stepped out on the edge for us. And He stopped along the way to pick us up. He didn't ask what sort of degree we had or what color our skin was. He didn't check to see if our grammar was proper or if we had enough money. He is a cutting-edge Savior with a cutting-edge ministry. And He is my Hero.

Chapter 5

THE CUTTING-EDGE CHURCH: Possessed by the Spirit of God

What exactly is the "cutting-edge church"? When I think of biblical cutting-edge people, my thoughts go to people like Haggai and Zechariah, the prophets and leaders used in the restoration of the remnant of God's covenant people. Focused on rebuilding the nation, these two men moved out toward accomplishing the vision, but the wrong people wanted a piece of the action. When they couldn't get it, they devised false testimony against them. (See Ezra 4–5.) The enemy's entire strategy was to frustrate the men's purpose. It is recorded in Ezra 4:24 that the work ceased for a time; it was stopped by man's power and might. But that which has been authored by the Spirit of God cannot be stopped forever. It shall be revived!

"BY MY SPIRIT," SAYS THE LORD

Haggai and Zechariah had to step out of yesterday and into today. As soon as the prophets heard from the Lord, they began to build again; Ezra 6 testifies to the accomplishment of their mission. These men of God stepped out on the cutting edge and fulfilled God's calling.

There are modern-day Haggais and Zechariahs being called to
revive that which has been hindered by man's power and might. In
the late 1990s we began to see a restored effort to revive the local
church. Some might think it began previously to this, but what we felt
prior to that was the release of the Breath of God, stirring the prophetic anointing, which we know serves to illuminate, reveal, and send
forth.

When we stop and think about it, doesn't it make sense that God
birthed the Church by sending His only begotten Son? The Church
and what we read about in the epistles is God-breathed and birthed by
His Spirit. The adversary uses people to thwart the purposes of God,
but Zechariah 4:6b declares, "Not by might, nor by power, but by My
spirit, saith the Lord of hosts." There is an all-out call from God for
those who will step out to rebuild, restore, and revive. The Lord is
searching for those who will respond in spite of hindrances. But we
must remember this: We cannot accomplish anything in our own
strength. God desires to rebuild the foundation of the Church and
bring revival to humanity, but that will happen only as we learn to
lean on His strength and not our own.

The first thing to remember, then, is that the true cutting-edge
person, church, or ministry operates by the power of Ruach Ha
Kodesh. *All things authored by the Spirit must be operated by the
Spirit.* Second, we also must remember that everything authored by
the Spirit, even if it's been damaged or hampered by human interfer-
ence, has the potential of being revived. If a church has seemingly lost
its life, it can be revived. If the pastor feels he can't preach anymore,
that the messages are not what they should be, the gifting can still be
revived. If believers feel they have lost their fire, it can be revived—
because *that which is authored by God cannot stay dead.* God is in the
resurrection business! The enemy wants to frustrate God's plans and
purposes; he wants to get believers off course. But he can't stop the
work of God. He may seemingly do so temporarily, as was the case
with Haggai and Zechariah, but he didn't permanently stop the work
God had purposed. If it's God's work, it won't stay dead. The Spirit of
God will revive and accomplish it.

Risky Business

All of us, to one degree or another, are risk takers. But what exactly does that mean? To take a risk is to deal with some degree of uncertainty; if the outcome were certain, there would be no risk. When an insurance company issues someone a policy, it takes a risk. When we buy a used car, we take a risk. When we get married, we take a risk. When we co-sign for a loan, we take a risk. To take a risk means there is a probability or uncertainty factored into the situation that may not be apparent at the moment.

The uncertainty of the particular risk involved is what holds many of us back from stepping out on the cutting edge. The devil plays on our fear of the unknown to keep us from entering in to what God has for us. The last thing in the world satan wants is to see biblical prophecy fulfilled, and he knows our stepping out onto the cutting edge will accomplish just that.

Uncertainty over things we don't know can intimidate us, but we can get past our fears of the unknown when we concentrate on those things we *do know*. For instance, I know the Lord said in Luke 19:13 to occupy till He comes. I know the Lord said in First John 4:4 that He who is in us is greater than he who is in the world. I know because of what I read in Psalm 91:1 that if I dwell in the secret place of the Most High, He will cover and protect me with His shadow. I know because of the words of Isaiah 59:19 that when the enemy comes in like a flood, the Lord lifts up a standard against him. I know from the promises in Mark 16:18 and Luke 10:19 that I have authority to trample on serpents and scorpions and over all the power of the enemy, and nothing will hurt me. I know I have been breathed upon by Ruach Ha Kodesh, and there is power in the blood of my Jesus. I may not know how the world or even the Church will respond to my stepping out onto the edge, but I do know this: When I step out, I will not be alone. My God will be with me, He will protect me, and He will fulfill His purpose in and through me. And that is all I need to know.

When we take a risk in our service to God, the risk is with humanity, never with God. Neither is the risk with the devil, since we already are involved in a spiritual war with him. Therefore, the challenge is to get past the point of caring what people think or say about us. Then we'll be ready to step out on the edge. But to get there requires a surrender that causes us to be more concerned with what God sees when He looks at us than what other people see. And that's risky business!

John the Baptist went forth in the spirit and power of Elijah. He was called on by God to be a voice crying in the wilderness, making ready a people prepared for the Lord. This was a cutting-edge man of God. Every time God gets ready to make history, He presents us with risky business. Today there are people all over this planet taking risks for the sake of the gospel—risks as radical as walking away from relationships or losing their lives through persecution. But they move ahead because they know they are taking part in today, leaving yesterday behind. I have often said that serving God is adventurous. Every day is a new day with God. It doesn't matter if it seems we are repeating the same thing time and again; there is something about the involvement of the Spirit of the Lord that makes the familiar fresh and new.

John the Baptist risked—and eventually forfeited—his life by telling Herod and Herodias that their immorality was wrong. (See Matthew 14:1-12.) He could have limited his ministry to baptizing and crying out prophetically, which was risky business enough. But God called John to step out even further—and he responded.

For most of us, risky business may not mean giving up our lives as martyrs. But whatever God calls us to, it's worth the risk because there's nothing like seeing blind eyes opened, lame folks walking, demonized people set free, and hungry souls running to the altar to surrender their lives to God. When we take the risk, when we step out on the edge and obey God, miracles will follow. We can't allow fear to hold us back from being a part of what God is doing in the earth today. We must trust Him because He's true to His Word. There are no uncertainties with God, and if we'll take the risk for Him, He'll lift up a standard for us.

STANDING IN THE PRESENCE OF TOMORROW

For years I taught on the subject of deliverance. When dealing with individuals, we must realize there are two types of demonic strongholds. There's the rational stronghold, where people in bondage believe they have the right to behave and think as they do, so they refuse help. Then there's the irrational stronghold, where people feel they're wrong but don't know how to deal with their problems and seek deliverance. Dealing with the rational stronghold is much more difficult because the problems are usually buried under hidden fears that keep the person from receiving deliverance. Although any kind of demonic stronghold is a horrible thing, to know that a person sees it as irrational is a good start for deliverance.

One of the biggest roadblocks to deliverance within the church is the "religious traditionalist." Many of the people shying away from cutting-edge ministry have wonderful hearts and really believe they're doing the right thing, but they don't realize they're stifling the Ruach Ha Kodesh. For example, a religious traditionalist might demand that the worship service be planned only from classical hymnal books. Now I love the old hymns, but that doesn't mean we shouldn't sing new ones. Other religious traditionalists won't read or listen to any version of the Bible other than the King James. I prefer this version and use it in ministry, but I'm certainly open to hearing preachers or teachers who use other versions. These are just two examples of the religious traditionalist's mind-set, but the important thing is to understand the depth of that mind-set.

In the previous chapter on the heroes of the faith, I addressed *pela*, or ancestral faith. The people discussed in that chapter were not afraid to stand in the presence of tomorrow, for *to stand in the **real today** is to stand in the presence of tomorrow. To hold on to yesterday is to refuse tomorrow.* Faith is the opposite of fear. Faith will embrace today, which brings tomorrow.

There is a hidden fear in many pastors, leaders, and churchgoers. We might call these people "religious traditionalists." Most of these people are unaware of their fear. Some of these traditionalists might be pastors who hold on tightly to certain traditions because they want to make sure they aren't leading their people away from God. For them, to leave yesterday is, in their minds, to leave God. They love the Lord so much they fear any change that might separate them from God and from what has worked for them all along. Now, I believe there's a time and place for traditions. Personally, I love Jewish tradition—not those man-made bondages that Jesus addressed, but the beauty of the biblical traditions that brings deeper understanding to God's Word.

But traditions, however valid or beautiful, can't take the place of the life-giving Breath of God.

People driven by what is often deemed a religious spirit are bound by rational strongholds that are difficult to deal with. These people refuse to think they could be wrong, and they cause numerous problems in the Body of Christ. They, as well as others who are afraid to break with tradition but have no rational explanation for their fear, need to repent and trust God to direct their paths if ever they are to move on in the things of the Lord.

God is calling His Church to step into the *real today*. We can't make today yesterday. We can't make today tomorrow. We must live day by day in the reality of what He is doing in and through His Church at that moment in time. This doesn't mean the past was wrong or not good enough; it simply illustrates the truth that there's a constant progressive move of God. Moses worshiped one way and David another, yet both were right. The rabbis did it one way and Jesus did it another, yet He did not tell them the Law was wrong. He told them their hearts were wrong. He also made it clear that it was a new day. Peter had to accept Paul, even though they were different. One believed he must become as all men that he might win one; the other held on for a while to yesterday. (See First Corinthians 9:19-23 and Galatians 2:11-21.) Peter didn't have a religious spirit, but I do believe there was a hidden fear deep within him. To his way of thinking, to leave the old ways behind was to leave the God of Israel, and even the Messiah, the One with whom he had walked.

In teaching on the Breath of God, the Lord showed me the reality of today. Today is where God is active. He's not active in yesterday; nor is He active in tomorrow. He's active today, which is the very essence of tomorrow. Our ignorance of what God is doing today has driven many away from the cutting edge. For example, I have had men of God approach me after sitting in several services where I ministered and ask my forgiveness for what they had previously thought about women ministers. Most will finish with a comment similar to this one: "I was always told it was wrong, and I didn't want to offend the Lord." How many women, called and anointed by God, have not stepped out in certain areas of service to Him because the ignorance of many in the Church said it was wrong for them to do so?

Not everyone who has a problem with change or transitional moves of God is bound by religious spirits. Those who are, however, are easily recognizable because they constantly lobby their opinions and sow discord and confusion among God's people. When we accept the *real today* and stop making excuses for what God is doing in it, we step into the presence of tomorrow—and that is stepping out on the cutting edge. God is doing a *new thing.* He is doing it *today*, not *yesterday*—and He challenges us to *know* it, or be a part of it. (See Isaiah 43:19.) The Lord is breathing upon His Church, and we are being called, by the grace of God, to respond.

THE NEW FASHION

There is a story in the Gospel of Mark about Christ healing a man with palsy. Mark 2:12 reads, "And immediately he arose, took up the bed, and went forth before them all; insomuch that they were all amazed, and glorified God, saying, *We never saw it on this fashion.*" This man with palsy could not even move. He was paralyzed and despondent, yet Jesus told him to get up. Those around the man watched in utter amazement. As the paralyzed man arose in response to Jesus' words, the spectators had to make a choice: *They could stand in the past with all its prejudices, or they could recognize the real today and step into the presence of tomorrow.* Every time God moves, someone is called upon to make a decision. Will we hang on to yesterday, or will we realize the real today and step into the presence of tomorrow?

The people who witnessed this great healing of the palsied man had never seen anything like it; they had never seen it in "this fashion." It was a new move of God; He was doing a "new thing," and He was challenging the people to "know it."

Today we accept many things our father Abraham might have had a hard time receiving. He might not have wanted to get on an airplane, let alone attend a service where everyone was dancing and shouting. Just maybe those things wouldn't have made sense to him. Even our custom or fashion of speaking would have seemed odd to him. If he had witnessed a Pentecostal church service he might even have thought, *I don't think this place is for me.* These would have been "new things" to him, but would that necessarily have meant they were "wrong" things?

The man with a withered hand, though he had no strength in that hand, was told by Jesus to "stretch it out." (See Matthew 12:9-13.) Sometimes, when there is no strength or faith in us, God tells us to stretch it out anyway. This is *pela*, ancestral faith. Once again, the people of God are stirring. Those with irrational bondages are being set free and are walking away rejoicing in the new move of God. Those with rational bondages (religious spirits) are walking away, prepared to destroy the Church, if they must, to hold on to their ways. In the days when Jesus walked the earth, these religious spirits wanted to kill the One who dared to introduce a "new thing." They were much more concerned with affirming themselves and hanging on to their way of life than they were in knowing or being a part of what God was doing. They were a stiff-necked people, living in bondage and subjecting others to that same bondage, rationalizing everything they did.

When the Bible speaks of "fashion," it speaks of appearance or the manner in which something is done. Jesus, though He honored the Law, challenged the status quo and showed the power of God in a way the people had never seen before. He presented them with an impossible possibility. It was a new fashion, and the people weren't sure what to make of it.

When something new comes on the scene, we must be sure it lines up with Scripture before we label it as being "of God." But we also must remember that God's Spirit is progressive, taking us from glory to glory. The message of salvation, the grace and the love of God, as well as His sanctified, powerful Word, will never change. But people and generations do change, and God deals with us accordingly. And with the passing of time, we get closer and closer to the unveiling of the King. I believe the measure of anointing has increased for just such a time as this. I believe God's people are noticing the "new fashion," and I believe God is looking for those who will step into it. Those who followed Jesus in His earthly ministry were stepping out on the edge. But Jesus said in John 16:7, "It is expedient for you that I go away." In essence He was saying, "I am releasing My Spirit upon My departure, that I might send you as My Father sent Me." We are *sent* by Ruach Ha Kodesh, called to step out onto the edge, into the presence of tomorrow.

A church on the cutting edge is one that steps into God's plan and desire, regardless of consequences or challenges. It is not necessarily a huge church, although it can be; it is one that makes a decision to step into the presence of tomorrow, one that will make changes, whether or not things already are going well. This type of church has a fresh anointing, and it will emanate love and draw people to the altars.

DISTINCTION AND PURPOSE

Just as all believers have certain distinctions, so do all churches. The key for all of us is to learn to operate within our distinctions. To be distinct is to have a mark that makes each of us different from others. There are natural distinctions, and there are spiritual distinctions. Natural distinctions are the obvious physical features, mannerisms, etc. Spiritual distinctions include our gifts, callings, anointing, and spiritual strengths. The big question is this: How do our spiritual distinctions develop in us?

I talked in previous chapters about impartations. An impartation is something that is given or passed on to one person from another. There are countless examples of impartations in the Bible. In Second Timothy 1:6 the apostle Paul charged his spiritual son Timothy to "stir up" the gift of God that was imparted to him by the laying on of Paul's hands. Impartations are real; they are genuine. But wherever there is a genuine, we will find counterfeits. Often people will try to imitate what they see in those they admire, declaring that person's gift to have been "imparted" to them, simply because they begin to look or act like the person they admire. However, as a rule, receiving an impartation doesn't necessarily mean we begin to minister like someone else.

My very first pastor was Dr. Jack Hayford. As a new believer, I could hardly wait to go to church because each time I was there I learned so much. One day Pastor Jack was laying hands on people in the congregation to receive the baptism of the Holy Spirit. I was among that group of people, and I *know* something very meaningful took place that day. As I continued to sit under Pastor Jack's teaching and my interest for ministry was stirred, I would listen to him and think, *Lord, I can never sound like that. He's an awesome teacher!* The Lord finally spoke to me one day and said, "Daughter, I have made you just the way I want you—distinct. I bid you, be yourself."

I can't teach like Pastor Jack, but I sat under his teaching for four years. During that time something I needed was imparted to me: balance and order. I've sat under the teachings and ministries of Presbyterians, Baptists, Pentecostals, and other high profile, respected Christian leaders, and from each I was imparted exactly what I needed. But this doesn't mean I speak or act like those preachers and teachers when I minister. We're all different "filters" for the Breath of God. My personality is different than Pastor Jack's or Pat Robertson's, but I received valuable impartations from each of them as I came under their leadership.

- Although I know there are different schools of thought, impartations usually do one of two things:
- Stir that which is already in us, or
- Deposit new spiritual gifts in us.

In most cases, when we receive an impartation we also receive a refreshing on our anointing. Receiving an impartation also can be a time of anointing or setting apart or stepping into an office or ministry, depending upon the measure God desires to give us. It may or may not mean we receive the same gift as the person imparting that gift to us, but we can rest assured that any impartation from God will give to us exactly what we need spiritually. To attempt to copy or imitate something or someone is not operating in the cutting-edge anointing. I believe I have received several real prophetic thrusts over the years, as well as some awesome teaching by example. But there's only one person with whom I minister in a similar fashion. From all the others I received what God knew I needed at that time. In some cases, I felt as if I was being "promoted" in an area of ministry.

The hunger for more impartation has caused people to do some strange things. Imitation may be the highest form of flattery, but we are to imitate Jesus, not other ministers. I'm not saying there can't be similarities in ministry styles, but God made us individuals. Therefore, our individuality—not someone else's—should be evident in our ministry. When we first begin in ministry and/or fulfilling our call, we can easily get sidetracked and find ourselves mimicking others because their method seems to work for them. Churches try it, people try it, ministries try it—but sooner or later the imitation is exposed. If we are serious about God and the ministry to which He has called us, we will repent and move on into what He has prepared for us individually.

Take, for example, fishing nets. One net is meshed a particular way and is meant to be used in shallow water in order to catch all the fish around the edge. Another net is made much longer for the purpose of surrounding and catching an entire school of fish; yet another net is designed for deep waters. So it is with individuals and individual churches. In Matthew 4:19 Jesus said, "Follow Me, and I will make you fishers of men." In everything God does, there is distinction—and there is purpose. Fishing nets have their own distinct meshing pattern, each designed for a specific purpose. Operating within our God-given distinction and purpose is what many churches and individuals vying for ministry are *not* doing, but we must learn to do so if ever we are to fulfill the Great Commission given to us by our Risen Lord.

A Review

Let's review what we have concluded so far.

- This is the hour of the fullness anointing. God is breathing Ruach Ha Kodesh on His Church. His breath contains the fullness of the Godhead. The last few generations have not experienced that fullness anointing, but God is looking for "perfect matches" in the local churches, those who will respond to His fullness.

- God is restoring ancestral faith, *pela* (the impossible possibility). This will move us out on the edge for God.

- There is change happening everywhere, both inside and outside the Church. It is a historical change, causing humanity to feel the difference as it shakes their insides. God is calling us to change things, even when what we're doing may be going wonderfully. We must review our hearts, our agendas, and our directions, even when we are successful. We will have to take risks to get out on the cutting edge.

- God is calling us to deal with the hidden fears within us, including and especially the fear of leaving behind the familiar and pressing forward toward the mark for the high prize in Christ Jesus. (See Philippians 3:14.)

We cannot be successful in ministry through imitation or duplication of someone else's distinction. We must be genuine, for the genuine will last throughout all our days on earth. Imitation will serve us only temporarily, and it will eventually be exposed. I believe the Spirit of the Lord is telling His people to search out their individual distinctions. He gave each of us a distinct ministry (fishing net). All of us are called to evangelize and to pray, but every individual, church, or ministry has a spiritual personality. Each of us has individual distinction, something unique and God-given. When we ignore that distinction, we stifle the anointing in our lives. I'm convinced it's our God-given distinctions that bring a mark of success on everything we do. For example, Pastor Rod Parsley has a distinction; Joyce Meyer has a distinction; Kenneth Copeland has a distinction. The anointing and impartation are real, but so is our distinction, each designed by God.

What is the difference between anointing and distinction? Spiritual gifts are recorded in the Bible. The apostle Paul said in First Corinthians 12:1 that he didn't want us to be ignorant. There is a diversity of gifts, he explained in verse 4, but the same Spirit and the same Lord. He went on to say in verse 7 that the manifestation of the Spirit on our anointing is given to everyone according to God's measure, in order to profit all. In other words, although there is diversity, there are many members of the Body of Christ walking around with the same gifts. This means that, while there are many operating in the same gifts and callings, there are still distinct traits.

Impartation isn't a license for duplication, though there may be similarities in ministries. The impartation is to be respected and kept pure. If we aren't gifted by God to teach, we shouldn't teach. If we aren't called to be pastors, we shouldn't be serving as pastors. God has called and equipped us *according to His purposes*. He is breathing on His Church, and He expects us to respond by allowing Him to search our hearts and by being willing to change things that might already be successful. To respond to Ruach Ha Kodesh is to take a risk, to expose our fears, and to move out and take our positions. It is to operate in our God-given distinction.

I, for one, desire a cutting-edge anointing with a cutting-edge ministry. In other words, I want to follow His direction for my life. The Breath of God will give us the grace to step out, stretch out, and surrender all, even things that may be going well. God will revive all that He has authored, according to our faith. He will respond to our response. We needn't fear what others think or do. We're marked for such a time as this. Once we've stepped out, we needn't look back. We can stretch out that withered hand with confidence, for Ruach Ha Kodesh will meet us there.

POSSESSED BY THE SPIRIT OF GOD

Because God's purpose for creation is perfection (drawing closer to Him), everything is progressive in our lives. In previous chapters I referred to the Breath of God as being "sent." *It is sent our way in order to send us.* This means that it is Ruach Ha Kodesh that is the instigator for God's purpose. Because we are to progress toward perfection (which will be achieved when we leave this world and go to be with Him) and draw closer to Him, there must be movement on our part as well as God's. We are the only species of creation that can make cognitive choices, and we can choose to move progressively or to digress. If we choose to move progressively in God's purpose, we move toward revelation. If we choose to digress, we become deficient in every area of our lives, and we mar our relationship with Him. When God breathes on us and we respond positively, we begin a progressive movement toward the desire of His heart.

From the beginning of time, all God has wanted from us was *all* of us—the real us, made in His image. Father God beckons us to draw close to Him so our hearts might be joined to His. The Lord watches us intently as we move toward or away from Him, while His heart aches in anticipation of the final outcome. If He can possess us with His Spirit, we become entirely His, transformed into His revelation, His glory, His image—creation as it was meant to be.

Making Disciples

Christians believe we experience conversion when we give our lives to Christ. Jews, on the other hand, believe there are two conversions: the first when one believes in the God of Israel, and the second when one decides to convert to Judaism, which brings the responsi-bilities of the Torah. Likewise, I believe there are actually two conver-sions in Christianity: the first when we confess and call on the name of Jesus Christ, and the second when we surrender all in service to Him.

As a leader it is my job to *make* disciples. As a Christian it is my job to *become* His disciple. As simple as this might sound, many in the Church stop at the first conversion and live their entire lives with-out ever surrendering to His Lordship and becoming true disciples. This second conversion, however, is what the Breath of God instigates in us to put us on the road toward perfection. We are illuminated and launched into wholehearted service to the Lord. This begins a process of changing, purging, and humbling. However, because this is a pro-gressive work, there is still much more.

Revelation

There's something we must always remember about the precious Breath of God. When a prophet received a word or message from the Lord, it was not the Spirit of the Lord that was the prophecy. The Spir-it of the Lord instigates and prepares the prophet to receive the depth of the revelation, stimulating us for that revelation. When this begins to happen in our lives, the Word of God *possesses* us. The Breath of God is the covenantal mediator that makes us a *recipient* of and a *par-ticipant* with God's revelation. But there is yet another step.

The message begins to burn within us with an intensity that makes it clear that it's not our own mind and will speaking to us. A transformation begins to take place within us because we're "hous-ing" the very secrets of God. We notice it, other people notice it, and God intends it for a purpose. Once this takes place, we have "attached" ourselves to the Son of God, and we live each day as though our very life depends on His Word—as indeed it does!

The Hand of God

Have you ever wondered what possesses a person to do certain things in service to God? I used to wonder that all the time. Now I under-stand because there are times I'm compelled to say something from the pulpit that I would never have said as recently as a year ago. It's the progressive work of Ruach Ha Kodesh within me that is bringing about that change, and I see it in others as well. The Breath of God instigates this process, and sooner or later we're "not ourselves."

The hand of God is the next step after revelation. When we speak of the hand of God, we speak of His might, power, protection, and judgment, but I'm referring here to the *pressure* of God's hand. First Kings 18:46 records that the hand of God came upon Elijah, and he ran before Ahab's chariot. Isaiah 8:11a says, "The Lord spake thus to me with a strong hand," while Jeremiah 15:17 says the prophet sat alone because the hand of the Lord was upon him. Acts 11:21 tells us the hand of the Lord was with the disciples, resulting in a great number who believed and turned to the Lord.

Once we've received God's revelation, His hand will force us to feel the pressure of His will, and we'll experience it whether we obey or not. When He gives us deeper revelation and allows us to feel the intensity of His Word, He expects a response. When we respond positively and progress as He's called us to do, we unfold His purposes and take part in the restoration of His image in creation.

This is the step that puts us on the cutting edge of what God is doing. It starts with the irresistible Breath of God, calling us to a progressive walk toward perfection. It is the crossroads of our lives, where we stop caring what others think or say and care only about obeying and serving God.

BECOMING THE REVELATION OF GOD

I believe each of us has three dimensions. The first is our *façade*, a sort of mask by which others perceive us, something we've purposely designed to build a certain image. Even the Church has a façade by which the world views and judges us.

The second dimension has to do with issues—situations, conditions, and problems we've encountered in our lives. Much of this dimension is hidden behind the façade; only certain people see this part of us.

Finally, there is the third dimension, the "real" part of us, the dimension that reflects God and that God wants the world to see. The devil can't stand the thought of creation manifesting itself as the image of God, lest blind eyes be opened with the light of His glory, so he does everything he can to keep this dimension hidden. But when we experience the second conversion, instigated by the Breath of God, that dimension begins to shine forth. Through the work of Ruach Ha Kodesh, God is restoring His image here on earth, and it is displayed through His creation.

If we wish to "become the revelation of God on earth," we must determine to allow Ruach Ha Kodesh to do His work within us, bringing our "real" self to the surface for the world to see. Within us is the glory of God, referred to by the prophet in Isaiah 60:1-2: "Arise, shine; for thy light is come, and the glory of the Lord is risen upon thee....and His glory shall be seen upon thee." God's glory shall rise upon us and be seen by those in darkness, but it all begins with Ruach Ha Kodesh. He is the instigator, the One who illuminates with revelation, then presses His hand upon us so we might respond to His love and passion. And He will capture us as a lover woos His young bride. Our response is not for the people, for our families, or for our ministries; our response is in keeping with a divine love affair between *Elohim* and all His creation.

When we become possessed by the Spirit of Ruach Ha Kodesh, we will be changed. We'll recognize the modern-day false prophets bringing a trendy gospel to fit our façade. We'll hunger for the true gospel, the one that speaks to the deepest dimension within us. We'll fear God and reverence His statutes; the smallest compromise will seem monumental. We'll be true disciples, possessed by His Word, obsessed by His love, and held captive by His Spirit.

Chapter 6

THE BREATH OF GOD

"Go ye therefore, and teach all nations, baptizing them in the name of the Father, and of the Son, and of the Holy Ghost" (Mt. 28:19). Under the inspiration of the Breath of God, Peter said in First Peter 2:9, "Ye are a chosen generation, a royal priesthood, an *holy nation*, a peculiar people; that ye should shew forth the praises of Him who hath called you out of darkness into His marvellous light." What did Peter mean by *holy nation*? When Peter wrote that verse, Gentiles were already being grafted in to the olive tree, along with the faithful Jewish remnant who had received Jesus as their Messiah. (See Romans 11:17.) No longer were there circumcised Jews only, but also circumcised Gentile hearts. Peter was addressing Christians, both Jewish and Gentile believers in Jesus. God had formed a holy nation, a nation made up of believers from many nations, brought together by the power of His resurrection.

A HOLY NATION

Something peculiar had spiritually been born. These people who made up this holy nation were peculiar because they were chosen and set apart by God, different from any other group of people on the earth. Others would notice the difference, and it would create a wedge between them, for our Lord Jesus came to create that wedge in order to bring forth a royal priesthood. In Matthew 10:34, Jesus said, "Think not that I am come to send peace on earth: I came not to send peace, but a sword." This sword was the sword that would set apart His people. When one is a member of royalty, there is a mark of excellence and separation upon that life. When we see royalty, we see a mark of distinction. Members of royalty seem to be consecrated for the good life, separated from the rest of the world. There is a seal of excellence over all they stand for.

We, as believers in Jesus Christ, are a royal priesthood with a mark of valuable distinction, consecrated for the truly good life— eternal life. The excellence of life is upon us, for we have been imparted the Breath of Life, and our breath is now of great worth. We are a renewed people, a holy nation, with unique customs and laws. Jesus brought a sword of division, not of unity. Swords do not bring things together; they separate. God's intention was to create a holy nation; thus a division had to be made between the wheat and the chaff, God's people and the people of the world. This separation would not be done with peace, but with a sword of division. The distinction would bring about a peculiar nation that was most valuable on earth. We are a holy nation, formed under one Head, Jesus Christ. This is the "mystery" of Christ and the Church.

THE FIRST ADAM

"And He said unto me, Son of man, can these bones live? And I answered, O Lord God, Thou knowest" (Ezek. 37:3). Genesis 2:7 tells us that God formed the first Adam of the dust of the ground, breathed into his nostrils the Breath of Life, and he became a living soul. Unfortunately, the first Adam fell prey to deception and polluted life with sin. As a result, there had to be a plan to save mankind from the destruction of the first Adam. Deep in the riches of the Holy Scriptures we find the plan interwoven throughout the prophetic Book of Ezekiel.

Most of us who have been in the Church for any time are familiar with the story in Ezekiel 37 of the vision of dry bones. In seeing the dry bones, the prophet Ezekiel received a vision of the condition of the first Adam. God took Ezekiel to a valley that was full not only of dry bones, but *scattered* bones, and He asked the prophet a *pela* question: "Son of man, can these bones live?" This was an impossible possibility! But Ezekiel didn't dare say it was impossible, for that would be limiting His God. So the prophet answered, "O Lord God, Thou knowest." The prophet saw the condition of the body of the first Adam, due to its sinful nature, disunity, and captivity. The Lord told Ezekiel in verses 4-5 how this body must be redeemed: "Prophesy upon these bones, and say unto them, O ye dry bones, hear the word of the Lord. Thus saith the Lord God unto these bones; Behold, I will cause breath to enter into you, and ye shall live."

Ezekiel looked at this *pela* situation, and it seemed impossible. The bones were dry and scattered—the very condition of the body of the first Adam—stricken by sin, captivity, sickness, and disease, a picture of humanity without Christ, without the Breath of Life. The question to the prophet then—and to the Church today—is, "Can these dry, scattered bones live?"

THE SECOND ADAM

In verse 7 Ezekiel wrote, "So I prophesied as I was commanded: and as I prophesied, there was a noise, and behold a shaking, and the bones came together, bone to his bone." There is nothing like studying the methodology of God. First He presents us with *pela* (the impossible possibility). Next He asks, "Do you believe?" Finally He tells us to *prophesy* upon the situation.

We discussed in earlier chapters that prophesying is not always done by one in the office of a prophet or by one predicting the future. Prophesying is the combination of God's heart, our faith and vocal cords, and the Breath of God, setting in motion something according to His perfect will at that moment. And, as we saw in Revelation 19:10, the anointing of the spirit of prophecy is the testimony of Jesus. Without this anointing, we're limited in our effectiveness.

When we're presented with the impossible possibility, the next question is, do we believe? Although the Lord knows our heart, He desires for us to express what He already knows because it's our expression that causes His response. Remember, we not only believe that *He is*, but also that *He will*. When Ezekiel answered God's question with "Thou knowest," it was a statement of faith in that this was a life or death situation, and only God knew the outcome.

Verse 7 records that Ezekiel prophesied as he was commanded. When we prophesy as God commands, we not only have the combination of faith, vocal cords, and the Breath of God, we also have obedience. We're doing as we're commanded. We're not speaking what we want to hear, but what He has commanded us to speak. Ezekiel prophesied as he was commanded, and as soon as he did there was a noise and a shaking, and the scattered, dried-up bones came together. At that very moment in time, prophetically, the second Adam was set in motion. A Holy Child was coming, filled with holy blood, and this Child would form a holy nation, a new Body under one Head. The scattered, dried-up bones would come together with His bones and form the Body of Christ, the second Adam. (See First Corinthians 15:45-48.)

The Body of Christ—the Church—would be gathered together *bone to His (Christ's) bone.* (See Ezekiel 37:7.) But even as the prophet saw the bones come together, verse 8 tells us there was no *breath* in the bones. The Lord then spoke to Ezekiel in verse 9: "Prophesy unto the wind, prophesy, son of man, and say to the wind, Thus saith the Lord God; Come from the four winds, O breath, and breathe upon these slain, that they may live." Once again, as we see in verse 10, Ezekiel prophesied as he was commanded, and the Breath of Life came into the bones.

But not only did those bones live, verse 10 says they also "stood up upon their feet, an exceeding great army." Why didn't the bones come to life when they were gathered *bone to His bone?* Why did the Breath of Life have to come before the bones could live? Jesus said in John 16:7, "I tell you the truth; It is expedient for you that I go away: for if I go not away, the Comforter will not come unto you; but if I depart, I will send Him unto you." At that very moment in time, prophetically, the day of Pentecost was being set in motion, when that rushing mighty wind, the baptism in the Holy Spirit, would give the disciples power to become witnesses to the uttermost parts of the earth. The Breath of Life would fill the second Adam with great power from Heaven.

This was different from the first time God breathed life into man in Genesis 2:7. This second blast of life released the fullness of the Godhead on a holy nation, a royal priesthood, chosen and separated from the world by His sword and formed under one Head—the second Adam, the Son of the Living God. When this took place at Pentecost, those watching marveled.

What was that Holy Wind that came upon the believers that day? Peter explained it this way in Acts 2:16-21:

This is that which was spoken by the prophet Joel; And it shall come to pass in the last days, saith God, I will pour out of My Spirit upon all flesh: and your sons and your daughters shall prophesy, and your young men shall see visions, and your old men shall dream dreams: and on My servants and on My handmaidens I will pour out in those days of My Spirit; and they shall prophesy: and I will show wonders in heaven above, and signs in the earth beneath; blood, and fire, and vapour of smoke: The sun shall be turned into darkness, and the moon into blood, before that great and notable day of the Lord come: and it shall come to pass, that whosoever shall call on the name of the Lord shall be saved.

"In the last days" is prophetic language that runs throughout the Bible. For example, in some places the word *today* can mean "the next thousand years." I believe the phrase "in the last days" to be prophetic, in that it could mean "in the next thousands of years." Peter realized that what they had just witnessed was *the beginning* of what the prophet Joel had prophesied years earlier.

This second Adam had been breathed upon by the four winds, the omnipotent power of the fullness of the Triune God. It had been prophesied in Ezekiel 37 that the second Adam would come together *bone to His bone*. It also was prophesied that after the gathering of the bones, there would be a release of the Breath of God on a corporate Body. Those bones, according to Ezekiel 37:11, represent the "whole house of Israel." Notice the word *whole* in that verse: "Then He said unto me, Son of man, these bones are the *whole* house of Israel: behold, they say, Our bones are dried, and our hope is lost: we are cut off for our parts." This word *whole* is the Hebrew noun *kol*, which means all. As *one* body, we are *all* parts of *one whole*. This word refers to each member of a given unit, of every kind or all sorts, coming together to form one whole, everyone who calls on the Name of Jesus Christ, no matter where they are from. This is the holy nation, the royal priesthood!

The Lord continued to speak through Ezekiel in verse 12: "Behold, O My people, I will open your graves, and cause you to come up out of your graves, and bring you into the land of Israel." Jews today believe that this prophecy is being fulfilled, as from all over the world they are returning to Israel. I concur, but I must also say, "There is neither Jew nor Greek, there is neither bond nor free, there is neither male nor female: for *ye are all one in Christ Jesus*" (Gal. 3:28). This word from the Lord is for a holy nation, a chosen and most valuable people, a *whole* people of all colors and cultures, all social and economic status, all shapes and sizes and ages. We are being gathered at the command of the Lord, as His obedient servants speak, and we are being breathed upon by the fullness of the Godhead—Ruach Ha Kodesh.

They Shall Be One in My Hand

Ezekiel 37:19 makes a fascinating statement: "Make them one stick, and they shall be one in Mine hand." To understand that statement, let's first look at Genesis 42-45, at a story about a man named Joseph. Joseph had ten older brothers who hated him because he was his father's favorite. Eventually the brothers sold Joseph into slavery, telling their father that a wild animal had killed his favorite son. With time, Joseph, who had been brought to Egypt by the slave traders but who, even in slavery, enjoyed God's favor, was elevated to a place of authority and power. Years later there was a famine in the land. As a result of Joseph's favored position in Egypt and his brothers coming to Egypt looking for food, Joseph was reunited with his family. God had placed Joseph in a strategic position in order to help his loved ones during a future time of need.

Interestingly, Joseph was the father of Ephraim, who was the leader of ten tribes, one of which was the tribe of Benjamin. Genesis 45:14 records a moving reunion and reconciliation, where Joseph and Benjamin, Joseph's youngest brother and the only other son of his dead mother, Rachel, fall into each other's arms and weep as they become one. Jewish writings declare that, at that very moment in time, the reunion prophesied in Ezekiel 37 was set in motion.

Psalm 133:1 declares, "Behold, how good and how pleasant it is for brethren to dwell together in unity!" There is something extremely gratifying about the unity of family. The wedge the Lord made with His sword was not intended to separate family—brothers and sisters in the Lord—but to separate His people from the sinful world. God never desired His people to be divided. He sent His Son to bring His people, His family, back together, even as Joseph was born into his family to be a son whom God would use to bring unity where there had been division.

But even though God's Son has come to bring unity, there is still division within the Church family. Christian denominations won't live and work together; pastors won't work with other pastors; brothers and sisters hoard their blessings; jealousy, envy, lying, and deceit continue today as insecure believers turn on one another. Why can't the Baptist work with the Pentecostal? Why can't the Presbyterian work with the Charismatic? Why can't churches of all sizes and backgrounds work together? The same blood of Jesus and water of the Word has washed us *all*. We are a holy (corporate) nation, marked and set apart for eternal life.

This brings me to the next part of Ezekiel's interaction with God. In 37:16, the Word of the Lord again came to Ezekiel, giving him prophetic instruction. God told Ezekiel to take one stick and write upon it the name of Judah (representing Benjamin/the house of David), then take another stick and write upon it the name of Ephraim (the son of Joseph), "for all the house of Israel." Then God told Ezekiel in verse 17 to *join* the sticks together so they would *become one in his hand*. When the people asked Ezekiel in verse 18 what the joining of the two sticks meant, God reassured them in verse 19 that it was all part of His plan *to make them one in His hand*. God continues to speak to us of that same plan today:

> *"Do you not know that you are **bone of My bone**? I will bring it to pass before your eyes. It will be a most moving moment in time. And to My appointed leaders, I instruct you now to take up the sticks and write upon them, as is your division. Place them in your hand, and the two shall become one. The people shall inquire of this, for they have not seen this before; and you will respond, 'Thus says the Lord: I will take the stick of the Baptist and the stick of the Pentecostal, and **they shall become one in My hand**. I will take the stick of the large church and the stick of the smaller, and **they shall become one in My hand**. I will take the stick of one nation and the stick of another, and **they shall become one in My hand**. I will take the stick of the worship leader and the stick of the musician, and **they shall become one in***

*My hand. I will take the stick of the Jew and the stick of the Gentile, and **they shall become one in My hand**. For I am making **one holy nation**, and I will be King over them all; they shall no longer be two, but one.' No more division. No more jealousy and envy. No more deception. I am speaking to My leaders, for it is in your hands I want the sticks. The healing is in your action, which resides within your heart. When the people ask you what you are doing, tell them, 'Thus says the Lord: **They shall become one in My hand**.' This is My plan."*

A NEW WORLD RELIGION

"For wheresoever the carcase is, there will the eagles be gathered together" (Mt. 24:28). It is accepted by most in the Church, and obvious to many who aren't, that the world is headed for a one-world government, a one-world dictator, a one-world religion, and a cashless society. Biblical prophecy on this subject, found primarily in the Book of Revelation, shall be fulfilled.

When I speak of the unity of the Body of Christ, I am not referring to the one-world religion or order; the antichrist is plotting that. Remember, Jesus Christ came to divide His people from the world; He actually created an invisible wedge by His life here on earth. No matter what order is implemented in this world, we as believers can never be one with it. This is why the ecumenical mind-set of bringing together all religions as one is an abomination to the powerful, holy, sanctified Breath of God. A Christian can't effectively pray with someone who is petitioning another god. God's people can't be one with anything apart from Him. This doesn't mean we hate the world or the rest of humanity; we know from John 3:16 that God loves everyone in the world. But as children of light we simply can't have fellowship or unity with those who dwell in darkness. (See Second Corinthians 6:14, First Thessalonians 5:1-11, and First John 1:7.) We can't be one with those who petition demonic forces and call it prayer. We're instructed in John 14:13-14, as well as in other Scriptures, to pray in the Name of Jesus. John 14:6 declares that He is the Way, the Truth, and the Life, and no one comes to the Father except through Him.

So it is, when I speak of the gathering, I'm referring to the Body of Christ, many parts and sorts of a whole, a holy nation, whose citizenship is in Heaven. Nevertheless, we love all people and continue to pray for their salvation and God's mercy upon the earth. Sadly, there are Christians who think they're helping to bring about peace by attempting to spiritually bond with non-Christians. That might work temporarily, but Jesus warned in Matthew 24:7 that in the last days nation will rise against nation and kingdom against kingdom, and there will be famines and pestilences and earthquakes in various places. Paul also warned in First Thessalonians 5:3, "For when they shall say, Peace and safety; then sudden destruction cometh upon them, as travail upon a woman with child; and they shall not escape." The apostle was speaking of the ungodly who will usher in the antichrist and the New World order. They will speak of peace and safety, and even attempt to infiltrate the holy nation. But in the midst of their fairytale, they shall suddenly be awakened to the truth. Unavoidable destruction will come upon them.

In Matthew 24:28 Jesus said, "For wheresoever the carcase is, there will the eagles be gathered together." The eagles are symbolic of worldly government, and the carcass is symbolic of the corruption of the people. Destruction will always overtake corruption, as the eagle overtakes its prey. No matter the attempt, corruption can't preserve itself from destruction. The apostle Paul continued to address this issue in First Thessalonians 5:4-9 by encouraging the holy nation, the "children of light," to be watchful and sober and to walk in surety, for God has not appointed us to wrath, but to salvation. Therefore, when I speak of unity, I need go no further; that which is undefiled does not attract destruction. When I speak of the great gathering, I speak only of the mystery of Christ and His Church, for we shall be one in His hand.

AN EXCEEDING GREAT ARMY

"So I prophesied as He commanded me, and the breath came into them, and they lived, and stood up upon their feet, an exceeding great army" (Ezek. 37:10). In First Testament times, when they spoke of armies and war, they referred to physical battles between real people. Nowhere in the Second Testament do we see Jesus participating with the political zealots of His day. Ephesians 6:12 declares that our battle is not with flesh and blood, but with powers and principalities, with spiritual wickedness in high places. When we as Christians speak of war, we speak of spiritual battles over which we have been given authority through the power of Jesus Christ. Many in the Church have prophesied that God is raising up a great army. How is this great army being raised? In Ezekiel 37:10 the prophet declared that the Breath of God was released and the gathered bones lived. First God gathered them, then He breathed on them, and then they came to life. Once they came alive, they stood up on their feet, and they were "an exceeding great army."

I spoke in an earlier chapter of our need for a correct response to God's Ruach Ha Kodesh. God is searching for those who will respond to Him. A response to the Breath of God is a perfect match for God. The body in Ezekiel's prophetic vision stood up after being breathed upon by God. As Christians who have received God's life, we must respond by standing to attention and becoming part of His great army. To respond to God gives us a status of perfection in His eyes.

Did you know that from the time of Abraham to the time of Saul's reign there was no formal army in the nation of Israel? When a crisis came they frantically called for able-bodied men to respond. All who were able participated in warfare. Israel did not have a formal military army until fairly late in their history because there was no unity among them, and the leaders were the primary source of the problem. The tribal leaders had their own doctrines and opinions, and they avoided working together. Even after some armies were formed, there were still problems with unity. From the beginning of time, leaders were responsible for the success or failure of their armies. An army consists of an organized group of warriors, trained in strategy and battle, and imparted loyalty, integrity, and a sense of responsibility. Without responsible leaders, a great army can't be built, nor can it survive.

I believe the Church has reverted to the days when there was no formal army. We talk a lot about "the army of the Lord"; however, we haven't had "an exceeding great army" because leaders haven't been in unity. If the leaders aren't in unity, the people won't be in unity. History repeats itself. When there is a crisis, able-bodied warriors are called in to assist in the spiritual battle. For years, the Church has survived off God's mercy and the help of those who respond during a crisis. But there has been no formal army. Now God is going to raise up an *exceeding great army*, in fulfillment of prophecy. He has already begun *gathering* this potential group of spiritual warriors, and He will breathe on them and they will live, but they will have to make the decision to stand up as an exceeding great army! It will begin with the leadership in the Body of Christ. Leaders *must* put their differences aside and work together.

The days of responding to crises and calling for last minute able-bodied volunteers are over. We need a trained and loyal army. God is gathering His people; after the gathering there will be a corporate Holy Blast of God's Breath that will cause us to rise up and live in the midst of chaos, standing together as an exceeding great army.

I believe leaders will be held accountable for their lack of sensitivity to the plan of God. They will be held responsible for the influence they have on their congregations and supporters. When leaders stand to attention, their followers do the same. God desires an exceeding great army, one that is trained and combat ready, not one that comes together at the last minute to try to avert a catastrophe, and certainly not one that is concerned with defending only its own little empire. God wants an exceeding great army who will take a stand for the *whole* body of Christ—*one in His hand.*

GIVEN TO ME BY PROMISE

Acts 1:4 reads, "And, being assembled together with them, [Jesus] commanded them that they should not depart from Jerusalem, but wait for the promise of the Father, which, saith He, ye have heard of Me." Most of us are familiar with those powerful and anointed words—*the promise of the Father.* Yet seldom do we hear much about the words that finish that statement: "which, saith He, ye have heard of Me." Jesus was saying that the promise of the Father is the promise of the Spirit, the Comforter, which He had already told them about in John 14:16, 26; 15:26; and 16:7.

I can remember when I was a child and wanted something specific, I would ask my father for it. When my birthday or Christmas was a long way off, he would promise that, when it was time, I would receive my gift. I was confident that gift was coming because I knew my father would never let me down. I waited with anticipation, and when the day finally arrived, the gift seemed all the more valuable. The reason—which I didn't understand as a child, but I understand now—was because *it was given to me by promise.* When my father told me he was going to get it for me, it created within me a dependency on his word. This has helped me to understand the promise of the Father.

God knows that when He makes a promise, He creates a dependency upon His Word, which is all in His plan. The heirs of His promises must be confident in the One who has made those promises. The promise is received by faith as we wait for that which He has promised. When the day finally arrives and we receive our gift, it becomes much more valuable than if we had received it immediately, without having to wait or yearn for it. Everything from the Father is given by promise. He wants us to wait in confidence, and value the gift when it comes.

The promise is received by faith through grace. The promise of the Father is the promise of the Breath of God, the promise of Ruach Ha Kodesh, the fullness of wisdom and understanding, the Spirit of counsel and might, the Spirit of knowledge and of the fear of the Lord. It is all degrees of the Spirit of prophecy, and it is enabling grace. Jesus instructed His disciples to wait for the promise of the Father, which would give them power from God. They were to wait for the promise, and cherish it when it came.

What is this promise all about? Acts 2:39 declares, "The promise is unto you, and to your children, and to all that are afar off, even as many as the Lord our God shall call." It is the gift of the Holy Spirit, the Holy Breath of Life. This Scripture in Acts tells us that promise was not just for the disciples on the day of Pentecost, but to all who believe, regardless of when or where they live. It is for you and for me. It is for our children and our children's children. God said in Isaiah 44:3 that He would pour His Spirit "upon thy seed, and My blessing upon thine offspring." This is not an issue of speaking in tongues; it is His Spirit. It is not an issue of miracles; it is His Spirit. I believe that miracles and speaking in tongues are for today, but that is not the focus here. The focus must be the fullness of the Holy Spirit, poured out upon His people.

The presence of Ruach Ha Kodesh was strong when Jesus walked the earth and on the day of Pentecost. We hear of people speaking in unknown tongues, of blind eyes opening, the lame walking, the deaf hearing, the lepers being cleansed, and the dead being raised; why can't we see it again in fullness? I believe we will, but the focus must not be on the miracles but rather on the Ruach Ha Kodesh, the Breath of the Godhead. Aren't we part of those who are "afar off," those to whom the promise is extended? Of course we are! But we must stop focusing on just the promises and miracles, and focus instead on *responding in unity* to the Breath of God.

Acts 2:1 tells us that the believers, as they awaited the promise from the Father, were "with one accord"—in unity. God's promise will come to us when we seek Him and wait on Him *in unity*. The Lord has searched for a responsive people—the perfect match— upon whom to once again release His fullness. This is the promise of the Father, and we can trust Him to fulfill it.

THE FOUR WINDS

Ezekiel 37:9 says, "Then said He unto me, Prophesy unto the wind, prophesy, son of man, and say to the wind, thus saith the Lord God; Come from the four winds, O breath, and breathe upon these slain, that they may live." There's no question that the promise of the Father remains in effect today. There's a rhythm in time that pulsates to the fulfillment of biblical prophecy. The rhythm has seemed to speed up lately, and all humanity feels it. The people of our day are frantically searching for truth, even as they turn to any and all forms of false spirituality. Defeat and hopelessness overtake them as they hear of wars, premature deaths, violence, and sickness. A demonic fear causes people from all faiths and cultures to look to any possible form of survival.

But there's a move of God's Spirit that even the world seems to sense. Notice again the methodology of God in Ezekiel 37:9. The Lord gave the prophet instructions to speak to the four winds, which are indicative of the four "corners" of the earth: north, south, east, and west. Ezekiel entreats the wind to come from every corner of the earth. This speaks of the all-in-all fullness of this omnipotent, omnipresent, incredible presence that brings life and grace. The prophet calls the Breath of God from the four winds and, in accordance with God's words, commands, "Now *breathe* upon these...that they may live."

This was a prophecy that applies to our days—the last days. Not only will we receive life from Ruach Ha Kodesh, but also enabling grace to stand to our feet, an *exceeding great army.* I'm not referring to the Holy Spirit that inevitably abides within us at our new spiritual birth; I'm speaking of something much more intricate for today. I believe we are experiencing a transition from the "dispensation of grace" to the "dispensation of the fullness of times," which *encompasses all* grace. (See Ephesians 1:10.) This is a Holy Blast coming from the four corners of the earth, the fullness of all in all that has been released by the spirit of prophecy (the testimony of Jesus Christ). God is gathering together in one all things in Christ, the Head of His Body, the fullness of Him who fills all in all. (See Ephesians 1:23.)

God is searching for a "perfect match" to respond to Him. That response must be:

> *"O Breath of God, come from the four winds in fullness, You who are full, You who are everywhere. **Elohim**, my Father, my Bridegroom, my Savior, You who breathes life and grace, breathe on me that I may live; and I will stand, my King, part of an exceeding great army. Come from everywhere upon me. Come from everywhere upon my family. Come from everywhere upon my church. Come from everywhere in fullness upon my ministry. Release Your Holy Trinity upon us all in these last days."*

As we pray this prayer and look expectantly to Him, ready to respond to Ruach Ha Kodesh, our journey begins—and it will be a glorious one, as we learn to "catch" the fullness of God for the fullness of times.

Receive ye the Breath of God.

About the Ministry

A Word from the Lord

"This ministry will go forth with the Holy Ghost
and fire. It will travel to all the ends of the earth and will
impart holy fire. This fire will act as a refiner's fire,
a welding fire, that will make many one with Me. And I
will be the One that will cause the hearts to bow and the
demons to flee, for I have placed within you a burning
holy fire that will well up in your bones; and I will impart
to others, through you, a fire that will make the disabled able.
Preach, teach, and prophesy. For that anointing I have
placed on thee will bind up the brokenhearted, proclaim
liberty to the captives and open prison doors to them that are bound.
Be bold; for I have called you a "trumpet" of mine and when
I say 'speak,' you shall surely speak. When I say 'go,' go.
I am your provider, your source, your power, your success,
your surety. Speak, I say, speak with boldness."

Given to Irma Elizabeth Diaz
July, 1995

The Vision

"To Attach Creation to Their Creator"

For more information write or call:

Upon This Rock Ministries
Matthew 16:18,19
P. O. Box 2146
Covina, CA 91722
U.S.A.

626-821-4182 or 888-567-7474
E-Mail: UTRHeadquarters@compuserve.com
www.irmadiaz.org

Books to help you grow strong in Jesus

Destiny Image titles
you will enjoy reading

▬ **THE POWER OF BROKENNESS**

by Don Nori.

Accepting Brokenness is a must for becoming a true vessel of the Lord, and is a stepping-stone to revival in our hearts, our homes, and our churches. Brokenness alone brings us to the wonderful revelation of how deep and great our Lord's mercy really is. Join this companion who leads us through the darkest of nights. Discover the *Power of Brokenness*.

ISBN 1-56043-178-4

▬ **HIS MANIFEST PRESENCE**

by Don Nori.

This is a passionate look at God's desire for a people with whom He can have intimate fellowship. Not simply a book on worship, it faces our triumphs as well as our sorrows in relation to God's plan for a dwelling place that is splendid in holiness and love.

ISBN 0-914903-48-9

Also available in Spanish.

ISBN 1-56043-079-6

▬ **SECRETS OF THE MOST HOLY PLACE**

by Don Nori.

Here is a prophetic parable you will read again and again. The winds of God are blowing, drawing you to His Life within the Veil of the Most Holy Place. There you begin to see as you experience a depth of relationship your heart has yearned for. This book is a living, dynamic experience with God!

ISBN 1-56043-076-1

▬ **ENCOUNTERING THE PRESENCE**

by Colin Urquhart.

What is it about Jesus that, when we encounter Him, we are changed? When we encounter the Presence, we encounter the Truth, because Jesus is the Truth. Here Colin Urquhart, best-selling author and pastor in Sussex, England, explains how the Truth changes facts. Do you desire to become more like Jesus? The Truth will set you free!

ISBN 0-7684-2018-0

Available at your local Christian bookstore.

For more information and sample chapters, visit www.reapernet.com

Destiny Image titles
you will enjoy reading

━━━ **HIDDEN TREASURES OF THE HEART**

by Donald Downing.

What is hidden in your heart? Your heart is the key to life—both natural and spiritual. If you aren't careful with your heart, you run the risk of becoming vulnerable to the attacks of the enemy. This book explains the changes you need to make to ensure that your commitment to God is from the heart and encourages you to make those changes. Don't miss out on the greatest blessing of all—a clean heart!

ISBN 1-56043-315-9

━━━ **THE LOST ART OF INTERCESSION**

by Jim W. Goll.

Finally there is something that really explains what is happening to so many folk in the Body of Christ. What does it mean to carry the burden of the Lord? Where is it in Scripture and in history? Why do I feel as though God is groaning within me? No, you are not crazy; God is restoring genuine intercessory prayer in the hearts of those who are open to respond to His burden and His passion.

ISBN 1-56043-697-2

━━━ **THE HIDDEN POWER OF PRAYER AND FASTING**

by Mahesh Chavda.

The praying believer is the confident believer. But the fasting believer is the overcoming believer. This is the believer who changes the circumstances and the world around him. He is the one who experiences the supernatural power of the risen Lord in his everyday life. An international evangelist and the senior pastor of All Nations Church in Charlotte, North Carolina, Mahesh Chavda has seen firsthand the power of God released through a lifestyle of prayer and fasting. Here he shares from decades of personal experience and scriptural study principles and practical tips about fasting and praying. This book will inspire you to tap into God's power and change your life, your city, and your nation!

ISBN 0-7684-2017-2

━━━ **THE RELEASE OF THE HUMAN SPIRIT**

by Frank Houston.

Your relationship and walk with the Lord will only go as deep as your spirit is free. Many things "contain" people and keep them in a box—old traditions, wrong thinking, religious mind-sets, emotional hurts, bitterness—the list is endless. A New Zealander by birth and a naturalized Australian citizen, Frank Houston has been jumping out of those "boxes" all his life. For more than 50 years he has been busy living in revival and fulfilling his God-given destiny, regardless of what other people—or even himself—think! In this book you'll discover what it takes to "break out" and find release in the fullness of your Lord. The joy and fulfillment that you will experience will catapult you into a greater and fuller level of living!

ISBN 0-7684-2019-9

Available at your local Christian bookstore.

**For more information and sample chapters,
visit www.reapernet.com**

Exciting titles
by T.D. Jakes

Destiny Image proudly introduces the T.D. Jakes Classics Gift Set

Includes #1 Best-Seller, *Woman, Thou Art Loosed*, and Best-Sellers, *Can You Stand to Be Blessed*, and *Naked and Not Ashamed*

With words that stand the test of time, T.D. Jakes' three books cross denominational lines, racial barriers, and gender biases to reach into the heart of the reader. With the compassion of Jesus Christ, he touches the hidden places of every woman's heart to bring healing to past wounds with the phenomenal best-selling *Woman, Thou Art Loosed!* With the same intensity he calls all men, women, and children to stop being afraid to reveal what God longs to heal in *Naked and Not Ashamed.* Only when we drop our masks and facades can we be real before our Lord and others. And with *Can You Stand to Be Blessed?* T.D. Jakes, a man of many accomplishments and life goals, shares personal insights that will help all people survive the peaks and valleys of daily living out God's call upon their lives. This classics gift set is sure to become a special part of every reader's personal library!
ISBN 1-56043-319-1 (Gift Set)

Also available separately.
WOMAN, THOU ART LOOSED!
ISBN 1-56043-100-8

CAN YOU STAND TO BE BLESSED?
ISBN 1-56043-801-0

NAKED AND NOT ASHAMED
ISBN 1-56043-835-5